CHAMPIONS' Creed

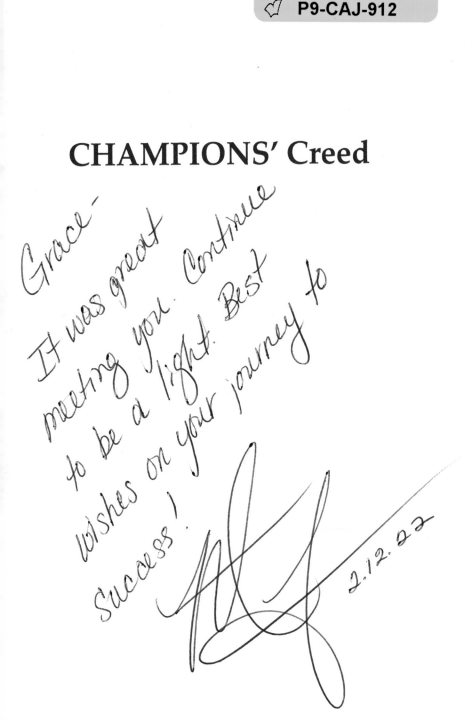

Grace —
It was great
meeting you. Continue
to be a light. Best
wishes on your journey to
success!

2.12.22

CHAMPIONS' Creed

Marke Z. Freeman

Marke Z. Freeman

Copyright © 2021 Marke Z. Freeman

ISBN-13: 978-1-7360480-0-9

Library of Congress Control Number: 2020948620

LIGHTHOUSE
PRESS

Cover by MASgraphicarts.com

DEDICATION

This book is for the little boy and girl trying to discover their reason.

It's for that dreamer in the class that's underachieving.

This is for the mother who had to figure it all out on her own,

for the immigrant who crossed those seas alone,

for the CEO fighting to keep the vision,

for the woman in the boardroom seeking respect and acknowledgment,

for the man living to break each generational curse,

for the athlete who refuses to be defined by their worst,

for the coach ridiculed for being uncommon,

for the individual seeking results but struggling to the find them.

This is for the first, the last,

for those struggling to escape their past,

for those doubted, conflicted, and convicted,

for all of those who feel limited.

This is for the influencer.

This is for the educator.

This is for me, you, them, him, and her.

CONTENTS

FOREWORD

I met Marke through a video she submitted as an applicant for Rising Media Stars, a program which was created to bring more diversity to sports broadcasting. The first thought that popped into my mind as my eyes scanned her resume was "She is already qualified to do so many things; she doesn't need this program." It's true. Marke has a vast resume with everything from playing sports, coaching, training, keynote speaking, and working nonprofits to being a CEO. She has touched every extension of sports you can think of.

As I cracked open *CHAMPIONS' Creed*, there was one thing I already knew for sure: Marke has reached so many corners of the world and has touched so many lives because she has an understanding of what it takes to be a winner. What I didn't know at that time was how seamlessly she would weave the various teachings and turning points of her life into lessons beyond the game itself. *CHAMPIONS' Creed* not only digs into the very fiber of how sport gives us the fuel needed to achieve success and develop character but it also gives practical exercises to integrate Marke's intentional and poignant lessons into your life. Not everyone who has picked up a ball, a bat, a golf club, a tennis racket, has taken the time to reflect on the kind of character building that happens in between the lines of sport.

Meanwhile, Marke has diligently collected and cataloged lessons on character, humility, gratitude, adversity, accountability, evolution, persistence, toughness, confidence, preparation, leadership, service, legacy, integrity, and much more. This book is for anyone who is starting a journey to greatness or is weary on their journey to greatness. *CHAMPIONS' Creed* is for people young and old who want to get to know sport more intimately including how its lessons can mold and change the trajectory of their lives. The storytelling keeps you guessing, and the exercises at the end of each chapter cement critical knowledge to memory to apply to our lives.

Before I started this book I asked this question: "She is already qualified to do so many things; what made her want to write a book?" As I closed the final pages, I realized the answer to that same question: "Because she can!"

LaChina Robinson

ESPN Women's Basketball Analyst

INTRODUCTION
THE BECOMING OF A CHAMPION

In an interview during the rookie season of my professional playing career, I was asked, "How did you decide who you wanted to be?" This question took me into deep thought and reflection. I paused and looked away.

My response to the reporter's question is the same today as it was then. "It was just that, a decision and commitment to be my best self."

All of us face the choice to rise into our finest self or simply let life determine who we are. Most people accept acknowledgments for their accomplishments without understanding that their journey shapes them into who they are, which is often different from who they want to be.

I grew up in a house full of boys and played on organized boys' basketball teams until high school. It wasn't until then that I realized there was a difference in the size of regulation basketballs. Most of my life I played with a ball that was 29.5 inches in circumference. In high school, playing with what others refer to as a ladies' ball, 28.5 inches, to accommodate smaller hands felt like the easy way out in my younger days. I now know better, but I was raised to avoid shortcuts.

That one-inch difference taught me so many valuable life lessons. I have learned that in life you cannot cut corners. If you do, you ultimately find yourself going in circles. I have come to understand that an inch can be the difference between succeeding and failing, between living and dying. Something as small as an inch shifted my mindset and pushed me to where I am today: the standout player, acclaimed speaker, notable author, and dynamic teacher.

A common saying and hashtag in the basketball community is "Basketball is life!" There are some who believe there is nothing more important than the game and others who consider nothing less important. I strongly disagree with both statements. There is much more to life than basketball, but there is also more to basketball than just the sport. In the game of life, you will face many character defining moments. At some point, you will struggle to find motivation, lack confidence or come up an inch short. When you aspire to be great, these are tests you are likely to face on every playing surface and in every profession. The answers to these inevitable tests are strategically placed between these two covers.

Some of my most eye-opening, vulnerable experiences are shared in these pages. If you plan to reach greatness, you too have odds to beat. *CHAMPIONS' Creed* can be your resource. As a professional basketball player at just five feet and four inches, this secret creed equipped me to stand out in a land where only the giants are praised.

There are no limits except those we set for ourselves. To this day I live by that mantra. This approach reaches far beyond athletics. I am who I am because of what I had to overcome.

"Who are you?" That question sparked this book. So many of us are not living the life we have been purposed to live. Our growth has been stunted by distractions, lack of clarity, and numerous forms of adversity. Some of us have been paralyzed by complacency. We do not have to live in mediocrity, mental shackles, or in boredom. We can and should wake up and embrace a sense of direction, fire, and desire to be a champion.

This book was written to show you that success is a decision, not happenstance. With authentic examples and results-proven knowledge, I share and unpack the nine essential characteristics needed to achieve greatness through an acronym I created that reveals the framework upon which CHAMPIONS are developed: Character, Honor, Adversity, Mindset, Preparation, Influence, Ownership, Nobility, and Service. CHAMPIONS' Creed is the roadmap to how I reached my dreams.

I have learned that champions are acknowledged for their accomplishments but defined by their everyday habits—something great leaders and successful teams and businesses put into daily practice. When you decide in each moment to continue to separate yourself from mediocrity, mentally and physically, success will follow. The rewards, acknowledgements, and trophies you receive are not merely the attainments of a champion. They are the confirmation of your dedication, passion and purpose-driven practices.

Several years ago, I had an encounter after directing a five-day leadership and skill development course addressing many of the topics we will discuss in this book. After ending our session with over 150 athletes, coaches, and parents, a middle-aged man approached me.

"Hi, Marke," he said. "I'm Michael."

He shared how much he had benefitted from my presentations, describing the information provided as "transformational." He added that his high school daughter was among the athletes served, and each day she called him feeling more educated, equipped, and empowered to achieve her goals.

"I had to see it for myself," he added. "You are a dynamic speaker, extremely insightful, and your ability to connect with the audience is world class."

He extended his arm to hand me his business card. "The mindset and the habits you have acquired through sports directly align with what is required to be successful in the world of technology."

He then invited me to come and speak with his leadership team. I glanced at his business card and immediately recognized the logo of a Fortune 500 company. His title read senior vice president. I looked back towards Michael in awe and thanked him for his kind words.

On my flight home, I reached into my wallet and looked at Michael's business card again. It reminded me of something I was often told by my mother. She always said, "You never know who is watching you." It's important to always show up. Success comes when preparation meets opportunity.

Four months later, I was on the company's campus providing training for their Supply Chain Development Program. Three weeks after my first visit, I was invited back to the site of this Fortune 500 company to serve as the keynote speaker for their Leadership Development Program.

The top leaders and companies in the world understand the value of the principles shared throughout this book. The concepts I introduce in this book have elevated the success of individuals, organizations, teams, and institutions worldwide.

CHAMPIONS' Creed was created to provide you with the tools you need to close the gap between where you are now and where you aspire to be—to offer the unbiased, uncensored, and undisclosed information required to maximize your potential. It doesn't matter if you don't know the difference between a free throw and a layup, the formula is the same. The truth is, you don't have to know basketball at all.

Mark Cuban, owner of the Dallas Mavericks says, "Business is the ultimate sport." He is better known for his leadership and successful investments than he is for his basketball IQ, but he openly shares how the skills required to be successful in the world of business are extremely similar to those in sports. I have learned the same. When we study the stories of greats past and present, we will discover that, though their journeys may be considerably different, their mindset and habits are nearly identical. We will explore the lives of successful people in a variety of industries. You must first be a student to become the mastermind. Throughout my life I have studied champions to help discover my own inner champion.

The biggest distance in the world is the gap between knowing and doing. To reach champion status, you must ACT (*Action Creates Transformation*). Throughout our journey together, it is imperative that you apply the concepts introduced immediately. Engage in each *ACT*ivity, answer key questions, and complete the daily practices provided. Practice does not make perfect; practice makes permanent. Applying these concepts will ensure that you strengthen your mind and transform your habits to achieve greater results.

When you are truly working in the intersection of passion and purpose, transformation is sure to take place and the universe will align with what you seek. It is important that when you take this trek through the *CHAMPIONS' Creed*, you approach it with an open mind. Be present and transparent during each ACTivity. Optimistically study the areas that differ from your initial way of thinking. Revisit sections that provide revelation. And, finally, recognize that sharing is caring. As you come across jewels, share the knowledge you attain with those in your reach.

Now is the time to activate your greatness and elevate your success! In this manuscript you will find the success playbook that supplies the daily habits and mindset required to reach a rare level of success in any and all respected industries—provided that you are willing to embrace the habits and live the creed. The word team will translate from the locker room to the classroom to the boardroom. Teammates are your peers, comrades, and co-workers. Leaders are not only CEOs and coaches but anyone with the power of influence. Championship level refers to attaining your ultimate goals. You will quickly learn that life, business, and athletics are not distant worlds. This creed of world-class champions is undeniable and never changing. Are you ready to become a champion?

1

CHARACTER

GOOD VERSUS GREAT

Greatness is a word used often but a level of success rarely achieved. Many define Michael Jordan's six rings as greatness, referring to him as the true GOAT (Greatest of All Time). Others would agree that the $152.9 billion net worth of Amazon CEO Jeff Bezos makes him great. I couldn't disagree more. Greatness is not defined by results. Wins, profit, history, and other forms of recognition are just confirmation of the many things that each of these high-performing individuals do greatly.

Greatness is defined as the ability to excel at an rare level in difficult situations. Though these two have had different journeys, there are many characteristics that are uncommonly common between Jordan and Bezos. Like all champions in their respected industries, their similarities are rooted far deeper than the fact that they outperformed their counterparts and sketched themselves into history books.

Their character transformed their results. Who you decide to be, how you show up, the thoughts you entertain, and the habits you have publicly and privately ultimately determine your success. These habits can be detrimental or profitable to your dreams. This unpopular truth is why greatness is so rare.

For those of you seeking to change your lifestyle or outer results, you must first transform from within.

Good vs. Great

Good is the biggest enemy of great. "This is good enough," has always been the phrase of the average being—the average student, the average athlete, the average leader, etc. Average means you are as far from the bottom as you are from the top. With the idea of "good enough" comes mediocrity, stagnant effort, and complacency. These three qualities have no affiliation with greatness. In fact, those who fall within the "good" guidelines often attempt to compare themselves to others. Comparing yourself to the majority is the first step towards mediocrity. Your counterparts are not your competition. For those seeking to become a champion, your greatest opponent is the "good enough" version of yourself. You need to attempt to kick his or her ass every single time your feet hit the floor in the morning.

Consistency is your target. This daily practice does not make perfect. There is no such thing. Practice makes *permanent*. All champions have failed, missed, and lost many times. Michael Jordan often shares that he missed more than 9000 shots, lost over 300 games, and missed the game winning shot 26 times throughout his NBA career. The difference between good and great is the toughness you build from your fall and the lessons you take from it. Do you always fall in the same spot? The worst lesson is the one that must be learned more than once. Champions fail forward, learning from their experiences and using their adversity as a stepladder to their goals.

Whether you are picking up this book to become a better leader, to find your purpose, to reach your aspirations or to improve the success of your team or company, all of these goals are dictated by the person you choose to be. To be great, you must do things others rarely do. To acquire different results, you must ACT differently and consistently.

I have had success that I credit to my failures because without failure you will never understand how to create and maintain success.

The world is built of three types of people: A players, B players and C players.

C Players are people who do less but expect more. The negligence they show toward their responsibilities is evident in their lack of effort. They typically struggle to meet expectations, lack coachability, and are mentally fragile. This limits their value to a group. They are typically found in the bottom 10% in terms of performance.

Next are *B Players*. They are individuals who typically have the "good enough" mentality. They usually do just enough to fulfill their obligation in practice and at work, and they leave on the minute they are scheduled to. They have little desire to develop personally and show up for those around them. B Players are found in the sea of mediocrity. That's the middle 80%.

Then, there are *A Players*, who are found in the top 10% because their presence is invaluable. They are not perfect but they are consistent. Their losses are never due to lack of effort. They come into the gym or office early and they stay late, taking pride in quality, coachability, and execution. Their uncommon habits are so contagious that it elevates the entire team. They are willing to go the extra inch or mile and do not cut corners. *A Players* possess a personal growth mindset and personal standards of excellence.

It is the people who thinks they know it all who know nothing at all, and the people who realize they don't know enough who will discover all the answers.

From 1981 to 2001, Jack Welch served as the Chief Executive Officer of General Electric. During his 20 years of tenure, he increased the company's revenue nearly fivefold. Want to know how? Well, he adapted a unique model that helped the value of company shares on the stock market to soar from $14 billion to more than $410 billion. Under the leadership of Welch, the company divided their employees into *A, B, & C Players* as described above. Each year they would fire *C Players* to rid the company of bad business. C *Players* were hazardous to the culture G.E. needed to create and be great. Their value was not evident, so it was an easy decision to make. *B Players* were more closely examined. They identified *B Players* they felt were on the cusp of becoming *A Players* and allowed them to keep their jobs. The other *B Players* teetering on the opposite end were let go. Lastly, they observed their *A Players*, the top 10 percent. They received raises, promotions, and other rewards for their outstanding work. General Electric followed this system annually, and each year their staff and results improved. Because of the company's commitment to employ only *A Players*, they achieved major increases in their results and profit becoming the most valuable company in the world. *A Players* are prolific. They are difference makers and irreplaceable. Be an *A Player* and build your team of *A players* personally and professionally. The results will speak for themselves. *Fortune* magazine named Jack Welch the "Manager of the Century," and *The Financial Times* named G.E. "the World's Most Respected Company" for three straight years.

Make your excellence the new norm.

If you are like me, you have been each of these players at some point in your life. You are not what you have done once; you are what you do often. Regardless of the player you choose to be, your habits determine your results. Strive to establish *A player* habits from this point forward. If you aim for the stars and miss, you have a good chance of landing on the clouds. Champions give their all in everything they are called to do. Even when they fall short, their character is still undoubtable. It is not *what* you do but *how* you choose to do it. It's a choice. Decide to be prolific!

Daily Practices: A Champion's Standards of Excellence

Champions are intentional in every action and interaction to maximize success. Standards are often the grand separator between good and great. Choose to be excellent in all that you do. This begins with the values that you stand on in every area of your life. Below is a list of five to thrive. Raise your standards and elevate your results.

1. Presence: Be exactly where your feet are. Be fully committed to starring in your role in each moment. Seek to contribute to every environment you are in, adding unmeasurable amounts of value through your energy, effort, and insight provided.

2. Non-negotiables: Live in a way that aligns with your high moral beliefs and intentions. Do not sacrifice the better version of yourself for rewards or acknowledgment. Stay true to yourself acting with a rare level of honesty and integrity.

3. Preparation: Have a growth mentality. Seek to be better each day than you were just the day before. Prepare with a student's focus and a surgeon's precision. Your goal is to consistently do things as well as they can be done, learning and growing from each success and failure.

4. Respect: Respect the process that comes with being great at anything. There is no substitute for time. Embrace the time it takes to evolve. Act without expectation but instead with great humility.

5. Performance: Consistently move with precision, moral integrity, and undeniable effort.

Greatness is a daily choice and an hourly act.

You are the Captain of Your Ship

Greatness does not happen by chance. You can't wish to be outstanding. You can't have one good performance and be great. You can't win the lottery and be great. Success is not defined by wealth or by wins. Greatness comes from consistency of character which creates reliability of performance and eventually consistency of results. It is earned! Who you were yesterday is never as important as who you need to be today. So let's start right here, right now.

Who are you? It is important to know who you are and what you represent to stay rooted. This question gave life to this book. Your standards make up your identity. These values or lack thereof are the anchors of your success or the Achilles' heel of your failures. You are the captain of your ship. You are in control of your destiny.

My mother was the best coach I ever had. The interesting thing is that she never coached sports a day in my life. In fact, she didn't know a lot about basketball until I began to play. Our conversations concerning my games were about character, not performance. Instead, she reminded me often that, though I was playing for the name on the front of my uniform, what was most important was the name on the back. In other words, what was most significant was not the number of wins I had but how I carried myself and what I represented for myself and others.

Our conversation had nothing to do with the game yet everything to do with the game. She would challenge how quickly I recovered when shots or calls didn't fall in my favor, what kind of teammate I was, how coachable I needed to be when we were losing, and how quickly I got up when knocked down. She would celebrate me for missed shots simply because of effort and constantly reminded me of the value I added as a person and a leader. She wasn't coaching basketball; she was coaching character and happened to create a standout athlete.

The success formula is the same. Because of these lessons, I don't believe there is a punch that life can throw that I can't recover from. She always allowed me to enjoy the game I loved and was my biggest fan whether I scored 40 points or zero points. She hugged me the same after every performance. She would grab me by my face and say, "Key, your best is always good enough."

Key was my childhood nickname, but she also used the word to reference success. You hold the *key* to your success. Your character is *key*. All were reminders of who I was. The character my mother coached is the reason I made it to my dream of becoming a standout Division I and professional basketball player. These invaluable teachable moments made me a Hall of Famer, but I would like to believe those lessons made me an even better person and leader. These are life lessons that can be applied in any industry. She never coached sports a day in my life, but she played a vital role in making me the player I became. These deep roots have defined who I am in my best and toughest moments.

Care far more about your character than your reputation. Reputation is simply how others feel about you. This is not consequential. More importantly, character is the truth about who you really are. This is always consequential.

Key Questions: Who Am I?

Transparency and vulnerability are extremely important when seeking progress. Don't run from areas where you can be better. We are all unfinished portraits. Choosing truth over harmony is the only way to transform into our greater selves.

Answer these questions with honesty in an attempt to self-reflect and correct. Who you are right now is not nearly as important as who you will become. It would be wise to keep your *CHAMPIONS' Creed* playbook close. We will often discuss questions that are key to your success.

1. Who do you aspire to be?
2. What detrimental characteristics will need to be overcome for you to become the greater version of yourself?
3. What will you accomplish because of this transformation?
4. How will others benefit because of this transformation?

CHAMPIONS' Code: CHAMPIONS are not achieved in the moment but long before—when we decide to do what is necessary to become great. We make this decision daily, in each situation, to continue to practice greatness and to choose to be the best version of ourselves. Success lies in the development of character. The results, rewards, profit, and trophies are not the attainment of the champion. They are simply confirmation of living the champion's code.

2

HONOR
SUCCEEDING VERSUS WINNING

I have been fortunate to work with one of the worlds' leaders in technology, a Fortune 500 Company with over 165,000 employees throughout the United States and abroad. As shared in the introduction, I was invited by this company to serve as a keynote speaker for their Undergraduate Rotation and Leadership Development Programs. If you know anything about the world of technology, you understand that it is highly competitive and forever changing. I've learned through athletics that dealing with a group of extremely competitive people can create a toxic work environment if not managed properly. A toxic culture can jeopardize the integrity of an organization and can quickly derail the overall vision of the team if individuals do not act honorably. Honor means to hold fast to uprightness or to a conventional standard of conduct with high respect and esteem.

One thing I share regularly as a speaker and consultant is the difference between winning and succeeding and the gap between losing and failure. There is no honor in winning or in failing. When seeking success, it is important for champions to understand and embody honor.

Succeeding vs. Winning:

Winning is not success! Winning is simply what is reflected on the score board at the end of the game. Yes, ultimately you want to win, but if you have aspirations of achieving greatness, you will define success differently. The determining factor of success is *how* you win. How did you progress? Did you sacrifice integrity?

When I was coaching college basketball, there were times when our scoreboard reflected a win, but as a unit we did not succeed. We didn't play at the level we were capable of competing at and we failed to stick to the plan. There were also times when we lost but were successful. We grew in the areas we were focusing on, we executed, and our effort was never in question. We just came up short on the scoreboard.

If your only focus is winning, how can you ensure continued growth? The champion's creed is a commitment to consistency. Whether we are talking games, quotas, or a friendly race, success is the respectability of the individual who wins. It's winning with honor. You want to succeed and to win, but you don't have to win to succeed. Success is more important than winning.

Losing vs. Failure:

Many people do not know there is a distinction between losing and failing. The difference is just as grand as the gap between good and great. I define failure as abandoning one's vision and values. It's giving up when things get challenging or not trying at all.

I grew up in a house full of boys, my brothers. As the second youngest, I learned I would have my fair share of losses before I would get my first win. Respecting the process, I spent many days at local park basketball courts getting my butt kicked by my older brothers. They didn't hold back and neither did I. I quickly learned the difference between losing and failing. Failing was mentally folding and losing was succeeding in character but just coming up short in score. I told myself daily I wouldn't quit, I wouldn't cheat, and they would not see me fall apart. I knew there was no honor in any of that. I stayed steady, competing every day, and, though I continued to lose, I was succeeding. I continued to improve defensively and sharpened my offensive advantages. After a while, I recognized that my brothers talked a lot less smack, which told me I was closing that gap. I was able to identify the strategies that made me more successful. I could see the strides I was making even when the score didn't reflect it. Growth is success.

I vividly remember a game during the summer before my ninth-grade year at Comer Cox Park. My older brother was missing his shots and I was making mine. I fought for every possession. I was knocked to the ground and I jumped back up. Fear wasn't an option. I was mentally locked in and my focus was undeniable. I earned my stripes by winning my first one-on-one game against him, and the entire neighborhood was there to see it. I didn't do the celebration dance that I had been planning for years. I didn't run home to tell my mom. I didn't throw it in his face. Instead, I grabbed my ball and continued putting up shots. That's the code of honor. It is how you win, not that you win.

You can lose and still succeed in sports, in life, and in the boardroom. Success is choosing the right way to win and sticking to that same code even when you lose. What you want to avoid is failure. Stay true to the champion's creed. If you face challenges distinguishing between succeeding and winning or losing and failing, ask yourself the following questions.

Key Questions:

1. How do I succeed in my position when the scoreboard doesn't reflect it? Have I remained true to my character and values? Did I give my best effort?

2. How will my character be defined when I win? What values must I stay true to? How will I show humility?

This champion's code of honor includes three vital qualities that every individual within a successful organization must have from top to bottom, bottom to top, and left to right.

Humility

True humility is understanding that it is less about you.

In 2016, I visited South Africa for the first time. Prior to my trip, I felt I had done plenty of research to have a foundational understanding of what to expect upon arrival until I heard these words from my native friend. "If it's yellow, let it mellow and if it's brown, flush it down... Oh, and two-minute showers, a splash before and after you lather; literally every drop counts."

I'll let your imagination make sense of that. At that time, South Africa had the worst drought the country had seen in 30 years. Throughout the southern part of Africa, the dismal rainy season destroyed crops, killed livestock, and even led to blackouts. Not confident when the drought would end, the country's people rallied. Those with more shared, and those with less used less.

I found South Africa to be a culture full of magnanimous beings. People humbly set aside their personal wants for the elevation of an entire country. Humility is freedom from selfishness. As I traveled through the city and townships, I passed signs from one corner to the next that read, "Ubuntu," a South African term meaning humanity to others. It also means "I am what I am because of who we all are." True humility for humanity. A champion's way of living. This is an experience I will cherish for the rest of my life.

Being a part of a business entity or team, we want to create a culture that supports all individuals as one, thinking of ourselves less as individuals to elevate us all.

Gratitude

Be grateful and you will find yourself joyful.

What if I could give you a remedy that could make you happier, mentally healthier, and more productive? If I told you it would cost you absolutely nothing, would you be interested? What if I said this priceless remedy was something you have access to at this very moment? Well, you have just struck gold, my friend, because I am giving it away! It is gratitude.

Gratitude is the solution to maximizing your lifestyle and value. It is an appreciation of the moment, the opportunity, the position you are in, where you have come from and what you are headed towards. As my mother would say, "It is counting your blessings."

You express gratitude by managing your expectations optimistically and leading or connecting with others and sharing a thankful spirit. Whether you see the number six or the number nine comes down to viewpoint. When you are grateful for the little things, you realize you have a lot. This does not come from a place of complacency. This approach of being grateful for the small or everyday gifts in your life has a direct impact on your perspective, which determines your habits.

When trying to reach an uncommon goal, there may be moments when you feel overwhelmed or powerless. Maybe you experienced a loss, your team is not on the same page, or you just have a lot going on. It is important to understand that energy follows your attention. When you lead with gratitude, it changes your mindset, which will transform your outcomes.

Will

The difference between the person who does and the person who tries is the person who will.

Will is the mental power you use to defy the odds. It is that determination to push forward when science, statistics, and critics says it's impossible. Though greatness is acknowledged by accomplishments, it begins with will. One must first *decide* to take on the insurmountable task and have the will to complete it.

Carol Owens, my college coach, is the associate head coach of Notre Dame's women's basketball team. In 2017, Notre Dame entered the season with a goal of winning an NCAA National Championship. To start the regular season, the team was ranked in the top 10 of AP polls. I had been following them closely for years, and it was clear that they were both equipped and prepared. Inevitably, this team saw adversity that no one could have expected. With a roster of 13 players, they suffered four season-ending knee injuries.

The first was their All-American center, the second was another starter, third, their top freshman, and then their first player off the bench. By January of 2018, their roster quickly shortened from 13 to seven players on scholarship.

When the dynamic changes, most teams alter their end goal as well. I followed nearly every game, watching them fight tooth and nail to the very end, sometimes coming out on top and also suffering tough losses. With their battered healthy roster of seven, the Fighting Irish, a team that had more ACL tears than they had losses, made an undeniable run in the postseason and went on to win the 2018 NCAA Division I National Championship.

I was able to catch up with Coach Owens on the recruiting circuit over that summer. While watching some high school basketball together, I shared the question we all would have asked.

"Coach, you guys went through so much this year. How was this team able to take down the best teams in the country considering all the adversity you faced and win a national championship?"

She responded, "Marke, our team changed [when players were injured] but our goal never did. We just told each player, 'You have to do a little bit more.'"

This was an eye-opening moment for me. It all started with the decision to be more and do more individually. Will combined with action is a lethal weapon. There have been countless stories of champions defying the odds. We must remember this: the vision never changes when facing adversity, but your effort and responsibility must increase. The will to overcome any challenge is the determination of a champion.

Champions face challenges head on, oblivious
to the odds.

Key Questions:

1. What does true humility look like for you?

2. How will you express gratitude today towards those you lead?

3. How will you show up when the odds are against you?

"The shortest and surest way to live with honor in the world, is to be in reality what we would appear to be." —Socrates

CHAMPIONS' Code: Champions take pride in succeeding, not winning. If we lose, it is with great honor and integrity. This part of the champions' code is one of humility, gratitude, and will. We approach each task with a magnanimous heart, a grateful spirit, and the grit to overcome. It is not a prize that is most valuable. It is who we become and those we assist along the way.

3
ADVERSITY
ACTIVATE YOUR GREATNESS

In Chinese lettering the symbol for the words *crisis* and *opportunity* share the same characters. The irony in that statement puts so much into perspective. When faced with an adverse situation, each of us has a chance to choose how our character will be defined. You can view your circumstances as a crisis, or you can see them as an opportunity.

Adversity is inevitable and it will come in many forms. Some examples are failing out of school, getting a divorce, losing your job, not making the team, or facing the death of a loved one. When you view your challenge as a crisis, you tend to question your abilities, find excuses, and give a little less, seeking a way out instead of a way in. When you see challenge as an opportunity, your mindset shifts optimistically, which creates a more positive perspective and directly impact your results. You eliminate excuses, you give more, and you think hopefully.

"There is nothing either good or bad but thinking
makes it so." —Shakespeare

I was born and raised on the side of town that most
tourists would probably be told to avoid. One of my childhood
hobbies consisted of searching the neighborhood for lighters
and shell casings that I could exchange for popsicles or
coloring books at a nearby fire station. I grew up on the east
side of Springfield, Illinois. I was raised in a single parent
home, spoiled with love, deep laughter, and countless joyful
memories. My mother and siblings have always been close,
supportive, and protective. This kept me close to my roots
once I stepped outside our home and was exposed to drugs,
violence, and other distractions in the neighborhood.

Growing up I quickly learned that everyone is battling
something. Some challenges are just more obvious than
others. For over a decade, I kept a painful secret. During my
adolescent years, I was raped. Because of guilt and shame, I
didn't tell the people closest to me. This left me in a state of
darkness. For eleven years, I couldn't even use the "r" word. I
felt like those four letters victimized me. I took pride in being
strong, independent, and positive, and this situation stripped
me of that identity and brought about embarrassment. I asked
myself questions like, "Why did you even put yourself in that
situation," and "How could you let that happen," as if I was
the one to blame. This dark cloud of guilt kept me shackled
mentally until I decided to see the opportunity within the
crisis. How I recovered was far more important than the
devastation I had faced. My desire to thrive in the midst of
my adversity gave birth to the champion I am today.

Activate Your Greatness

You too have a story. You have experienced something that could be detrimental to your character and the trajectory of your life as well. Build your empire with the same bricks that were thrown at you. All of these highs and lows become your power. When faced with adversity, realize that each situation is another chapter in your book. It's not how the story starts; it's all about the finish. You cannot have a *testimony* without a *test*. You can't have a message without sorting through the mess, and you can't make history without a story.

When faced with adversity, there are three types of people in the world: the people who quit, those who just survive, and the 5% of champions who thrive.

The Quitter is the person who chooses to walk away at the first site of frustration. The person who does not give himself or herself a chance. When faced with challenge in the workplace, on a team, or even in a relationship, quitting has become acceptable in many cases. It is now uncommon for a person to stay in one line of work until retirement. Not long ago, this was not true. In 2018, the National Student Clearinghouse conducted a study that estimated that 39% of all undergraduate students who initially enroll in a four-year institution transfer schools at least once during their college studies. Take a look at divorce rates in the United States. In 2020, statistics showed that about 50% of marriages end in divorce, and the number is rising for subsequent marriages. I am all for people living their best lives, but many seem to have a skewed perception of what is required to attain the lifestyle they seek.

I know that there are a number of things that contribute to these statistics, but I also believe that in many cases it has a lot to do with character. Aborting should not be the first option. When there is frustration, a lack of understanding or unhappiness, you must first ask yourself, "Is it a crisis or can this be an opportunity?" Quitting once makes it easier to repeat that behavior a second time, and eventually your life becomes a story of mediocrity. The habitual quitter never succeeds and the persistent succeeder rarely quits.

You cannot have triumph without a trial or tribulation.

I transferred after my freshman year at Florida A&M University—for all the wrong reasons. I convinced myself that I was changing schools because I was homesick and I would be better off somewhere else. The truth was that I didn't play much at the beginning of my freshman year. My coach didn't believe I was ready. Midway through the season, our starting senior point guard got hurt, and our sophomore point guard and I battled for that starting spot and for additional playing time. I eventually became a starter, but I knew that the following year I would have to prove myself all over again. I wanted to avoid that headache, so I left. Even after a historic season, I was seeking something easier and not giving myself a chance. Influenced by the fear that someone else might outwork and outshine me, I left a great university and opportunity because of my fear of doing all the work a second time and losing. If you are constantly comparing your story to others, you will never appreciate what your opportunities are preparing you for. To reach the top 5%, quitting cannot be your default.

There is a difference between quitting and moving on. People stay in unhealthy positions and relationships longer than they should because they don't fully understand the distinction between the two. *Moving on* means there is something detrimental to your wellbeing or there is no room left for growth. This is not the same as quitting. It simply indicates that you have outgrown the situation. A thorough analysis should take place. You must be in a healthy mental state to be able to differentiate between the two.

The Survivor does whatever is most convenient. They may choose to accept a challenge, but they will do just enough to get by. Their goal is not to excel; they simply want to get through the work. Examples include the student who does the minimum required to pass the class, the athlete who runs just hard enough to make the time, the professional who barely manages to meet the quota or the deadline. These people typically do only what is necessary to avoid failing and not enough to stand out. Don't settle. Practice succeeding; don't rehearse failure. Remember, practice makes permanent.

The Thriver is the person who chooses to excel in less than ideal circumstances. Show them adversity and they will show you their immense strength and mental toughness. They may feel an intense excitement to tackle the most difficult circumstances that life throws at them.

I have been the person that lacked purpose and persistence, which caused me to fold during a period in my life. I have been the person who settled for mediocrity and did only what was necessary to survive and not enough to stand out. I now pride myself on being the person who chooses to attack life's curveballs with heart, resilience, and optimism by finding a way over, under, around, or through anything standing in my path.

World-class Champion Russell Wilson was highly sought after to play Major League Baseball and to join the National Football League. On June 8, 2010, Russell was drafted to play baseball. Only one day later, his father and biggest inspiration passed away. He experienced his highest of highs and his lowest of lows just hours apart. He ended up turning down a professional baseball contract to attend college and play both sports he enjoyed. He came out of college the 75th pick of the 2012 NFL draft.

During training camp, he was told he would never last in the NFL and he was too small to play quarterback. These are times when the average person would fold, but through all the noise he continued to thrive.

On *Cold Calls*, Russell shared with Kevin Hart that he decided not to let these criticisms define his career. That wouldn't honor his father's memory. He dug deep and rose above what others had to say in order to move forward despite his detractors.

He went from being the third-string quarterback on an average NFL team to the franchise quarterback, winning the 2013 Superbowl. Now a seven-time Pro Bowler, Russell's greatest accomplishment has been not allowing his challenges to *define* his career but instead using them to *refine* his greatness.

Who Are You?

I found comfort in keeping my story secret because I did not fully understand what to make of my humble beginnings. Wrongfully, as a kid I thought being raised on government assistance, in Section 8 housing determined my value. I never wanted people to know of my father's issues with drug addiction and domestic abuse because I thought his actions and everything that came with that also defined me. I felt like I would lose the credit of being a strong woman if others knew I was raped. I was ashamed of my story.

Through my adversity, I came to understand that I would not be who I am now without what I had to experience and overcome. This is where refining takes place. I realize that I am not a product of my environment but a product of my choices and beliefs. The champion I came to be was created as my life was transpiring. The same young lady who overcame some of her biggest hurdles as a child also became the woman who established herself as an athlete, business leader, and speaker. I refuse to play or live to my 5'4", 135-pound frame. We must play and live to the size of our hearts, which is shaped by our perspective of the adversity we face in our lives.

Entering my journey as a speaker, I knew that sharing the uncontrollable, unforeseen challenges that molded me would plant a seed of hope and courage in others. My purpose and my greatness are greater than the pain I endured, and so are yours. Like yours, my story is unimaginable. It is full of trials, tribulations, and triumph. These experiences have kept me grounded and helped me distinguish between healthy and poor life habits. We always have a choice. Choose to be in the top five that thrive.

One of my favorite quotes by Writer Mark Twain reads, "The two most important days in your life are the day you are born and the day you find out why." Purpose is understanding your life's path. To comprehend your path is to see what seemed to be a loss as an opportunity to show off your greatness. My story continues to be full of life shaping opportunities. Even when you fail, have the resilience to fail forward. The adversity you faced from your earliest years to your current situation is preparing you for a greater good. This is the making of a champion. Your talents, your challenges, your circumstances, your purpose, and your triumphs are all connected. All are molding you into the person you need to be to maintain the success, relationships, and lifestyle you aspire to have. You must identify the opportunity. Character is created and refined in times of turmoil. Who are you?

Key Questions: Living on Purpose

1. Who am I now because of what I have experienced?

2. How does my journey add value to the lives of others?

3. How has this journey led me to my purpose?

Knowing who you are will help you discover why you are here. Knowing why you are here will help you discover where you are going.

What It Takes!

The best fighters in the world say they never get knocked out by the punch they see coming. It's always the one they didn't expect. A common misconception is that adversity is something that can always be anticipated. This false thought paralyzes people when they are unexpectedly hit by the truth because they didn't expect to be knocked down by life multiple times, sometimes in back-to-back succession and in unthinkable ways. In such circumstances, they may feel they don't have the mental strength to get up.

To overcome the battles that life presents, we must put on our CAPE and become Committed, Accountable, Persistent, and willing to Evolve.

- Commitment – Decide now who you are going to be in those times of uncertainty. By making the choice before crisis occurs, you are promising yourself you will thrive!

- Accountability – Take ownership of the things you can control and act accordingly.

- Persistence – Relentlessly pursue excellence.

- Evolution – Continue to develop in light of your circumstances and free yourself of the dark clouds from your past that still follow you. Break the chains of guilt, pain, and regret. Allow yourself to grow and step forward.

You will be challenged throughout your entire life and career. Your first test may be as a trailblazer, the second may be dealing with politics or unfairness, and your third may be failure. Just as Superman or Wonder Woman donned their capes before going into battle, be sure to put on yours. Who says all heroes and sheroes don't wear CAPEs? We all do. Some are just intangible.

It's proven that the path with more challenges is often the path to something great. That's the path champions take.

Choose Greatness

Success is not a destination; it's a journey. Growing up, I always felt like I resonated with Serena Williams' tenacious scream, Tiger Woods' fist of triumph, and Michael Phelps' famous smile of success. Some found their actions to be arrogant. I saw them as self-confirmation. I felt their determination showed in these outward signs of success. They embraced the moment as champions who had said, "I can overcome this, I will overcome this," and, finally, "I have overcome this." These outward signals revealed a combination of confidence, commitment, and courage.

Each of us wants to achieve greatness, but few are willing to take the path required. It will not be easy. If it were, everyone would reach the pinnacle of success. There is a reason very few in any industry attain that rare level. This path requires patience, rejection, failure, blood, sweat, and tears. Many try to avoid the challenges or shortcut their journey to the top, but there is only one way to greatness, and it's a path that true champions welcome.

Serena Williams, a childhood phenom, played her first professional match at the young age of 14. Over her 25+ year career, Serena has won 23 grand slams, more single titles than any other woman or man during the open era. She has revolutionized women's tennis with her powerful style of play but not without being criticized for her display of passion, body shamed for her natural build, and having her ability to sustain success questioned. Despite the mental and physical adversity, Serena is known most for rising to the occasion when the odds are stacked against her, when she is visibly in pain, even winning another title following the birth of her first child and recovering from unbelievable deficits to dominate her opponents.

Ellen DeGeneres is a comedian, actor, television presenter, and activist best known for her generosity and ability to connect with others. Many recognize her as the host of one of the most popular television shows to date and an advocate for equality. Very few realize that her earlier attempt at hosting

The Ellen Show resulted in being canceled after just one season on air due to low ratings. She received backlash after coming out as a lesbian in the entertainment industry. After those losses and challenges, Ellen returned with a new show and became known as one of the most influential persons in the television industry. *The Ellen DeGeneres Show* was nominated for 11 Emmys in its first season, winning four, including the Best Talk Show award.

Tyler Perry is a world-renowned producer, director, actor, screenwriter, playwright, author, songwriter, entrepreneur, and philanthropist. As a child he experienced abuse and molestation. He did not finish high school and found himself homeless as he attempted to pursue his career in playwrighting. Living by the words, "Don't give up," he became the mastermind behind over 20 feature films, over 20 stage plays, countless television shows, and a *New York Times* bestselling book. Perry has since built an empire that has attracted audiences from all over the world and built communities throughout the United States and abroad. He is now celebrated as one of the greatest modern innovators in the film industry.

Success is not measured by where you are. It's measured by how far you have come and by those you have helped along the way.

ACT: Choose to Thrive

1. Step Back - Observe and seek to understand how the choices you made and the experiences you have had helped to shape you today.

2. Step Up– Be confident. Take pride in choosing to be the best version of yourself, regardless of your past or present circumstances. Be more and do more.

3. Step Forward - Move on. Those are no longer poor decisions; they are life lessons. Commit to going forward, using your past as a motivational teacher. These are the moments that give your life, career, or position new meaning.

Creating the CHAMPION

As a sports analyst, I have been fortunate to absorb the knowledge of the best players, coaches, and influencers in sports. I had the great pleasure of interviewing Gold Medalist and NBA All-Star Vince Carter during the last season of his 22-year NBA career. As a little girl, I watched Vinsanity, also known as Half-Man Half-Amazing, demolish his NBA opponents with unforgettable dunks, game winners, with great integrity. He was the ideal role model, handling his wins and lessons with the utmost class. This taught me so much as I carefully observed his every move through my TV screen. I waited long after the game and passed up many interviews to speak with Vince. It meant the world to me.

Vince was just games away from becoming the first player in the NBA to play in four different decades. When I shared this news with him, I asked which decade was his favorite to play in and why? His response was compelling.

> *I can honestly say that great things have happened to me. Lessons have been learned in each decade that I still cherish. We think sometimes that we just want the good, but I think we learn a lot through the painful situations. Each decade, there has been good and bad, but it was all worth it. So many ups and downs that I'm grateful for; I wouldn't change a thing because I think going through it all still has me here today. Now I can share those life lessons.*
> —Vince Carter

Adversity is ultimately preparing you for your destiny. It is a key ingredient in the creation of the champion. Life does not happen to us; it happens *for* us. We must be battle tested.

Think of it like pressure. It can burst pipes or it can create diamonds. Decide to become a diamond. Choose to thrive! Life will never ask for our permission. We must prepare ourselves for character-refining moments and embrace them as we would the good that comes with life. Live in the moment, not allowing your past to ruin your future.

The only thing you carry from your past are the lessons. Leave the baggage. Your greatness is greater than any pain you endure. There is room in every story for a better ending.

Key Questions: Battle Test

1. What adversity have you faced that has refined your character?

    a. What lessons are you taking from those experiences?

    b. What luggage are you leaving from those experiences?

2. What qualities do you possess that make you capable of tackling your next challenge?

3. Where is your heart, resilience and strength to overcome your challenges rooted?

There are many things to learn from adversity that victory cannot teach.

CHAMPIONS' Code: A champion's past does not define him or her. It refines them. Their pain from the past has been transformed to fuel resilience and motivation. We cannot be who we aspire to be without these transformational moments. As a champion, we make the conscious effort to thrive when adversity is presented, allowing each moment to grow us mentally and prepare us for our greater good. We will step back, step up, and step forward because our purpose is much bigger than our pain.

4
MINDSET
A CHAMPION'S MENTALITY

The mind is the most powerful part of the body, one that can be your greatest asset and also one that can cause self-destruction. I have clients who are professional athletes, coaches, and leaders in well-known companies who find themselves being tortured by their thoughts at different points throughout their careers.

Everyone faces mental barriers—even the people you admire most. Different blocks show up at multiple times throughout your life. Those barriers birth the internal critic who forces you to question who you really are. It asks, *Are you good enough? Are you ready? What if? What will others think of you?* That mental voice poses thousands of other overbearing scenarios and debilitating thoughts.

The inability to control your mental state can be the most hazardous hurdle to your success. This can disrupt your dreams, your career, and your relationships. The mindset required to conquer an unfamiliar level of success is truly uncommon. When you study champions like Kobe Bryant, you learn that it was his mindset that separated him from his peers even at the highest level. In this chapter, we will explore the mentality that is limiting your growth and reconstruct the mindset required to reach an uncommon level of success.

A Champion's Mentality

Kobe Bryant possessed one of the rarest minds any industry has ever seen. His outlook earned its own title: the Mamba Mentality, also known as a relentless and an undeniable pursuit of excellence. He was a five-time NBA champion, an MVP, and an 18-time All-Star because of his way of thinking. From an 81-point performance during his career to an Oscar and an Emmy for his short film *Dear Basketball,* Kobe always set the bar high—even after retirement from the game that was his passion. Sports and film, two totally different industries, were dominated by one person and one mindset. It doesn't matter what space you occupy; the same mindset is required to reach a champion's level of success.

Attaining the level of a champion starts with your vision. The next step is ongoing: a relentless pursuit of excellence to achieve that dream. A champion's desire will not be denied. He or she has the will to go the extra inch, foot, or mile and the mindset to do whatever it takes and overcome any obstacle!

Vision

"No need for sight when you have vision." This powerful quote comes from my friend Lex Gillette, who is the best totally blind long and triple jumper in the history of the U.S. Paralympics. He is the current world record holder in the long jump, a four-time Paralympic medalist, a three-time long jump world champion, and an 18-time national champion. With no sight but clear vision, Lex has the resilience to overcome the many challenges he has faced since losing his sight at the age of eight.

Vision is something you can see with your eyes closed and does not require sight. Your vision fuels and guides you. It must be bigger than your circumstances. If it is stronger than your adversity, then your desire, focus, and perseverance will likely overcome any mental challenge, distraction, or setback.

The power of your vision and strength of your champion's mentality magnify your greatness, your ability to accomplish the unimaginable. Greatness is something everyone has access to but few embrace. It's a daily choice. I want to be the inventor of the first flying car; I want to be the first person in my family to graduate; I want to win a championship; I want to start my own software company; I want to write a book. Dreaming big is a good thing, but your "why" must be more important than what you have set out to achieve. Determine why achieving this means so much to you. Is it to break generational curses, to create generational wealth? Is it to change your program's history, or is it to provide a much-needed service to humanity?

Vision guides every decision. Whether you have the ball in your hands with ten seconds remaining on the clock or you're mapping out your life goals, vision provides direction.

You must write down your aspirations for them to become a goal. Once you have created the steps to achieve your goal, you now have a plan. You must *ACT* to make your goals and aspirations a reality. Once the vision is clear, it is time to MAP out the steps to activate your greatness and elevate your success. MAP is another acronym created to provide clarity and direction for high achievers: Mindset, Approach, and Performance.

The MAP to Success:

A. Mindset: Thoughts---> Actions ---> Results

It all begins with a thought. Your thoughts determine your actions and your actions directly impact your results. Whether that thought is positive or negative, it dictates the direction of your energy. Where you place your attention, you direct your energy.

In 1973, there was a man hired to fix a refrigerated boxcar on the back of a train. He started his shift as he would have done on any other day. He arrived at the train car, grabbed his toolbox, and began his day's work. While working, he panicked and got himself locked inside the train car. He began pounding on the door and no one responded. His panic worsened as he started thinking about freezing to death. To pass time, he began engraving his thoughts on the wall of the car with an object he found on the floor.

"I'm becoming colder," he wrote. His thoughts began to change and soon his body followed. He continued to write, "Still colder now. Nothing to do but wait." Then he wrote, "These may be my last words." And they were.

The next day the door opened. They found the man dead. Forensic specialists could not understand how he had died. The temperature was at 56 degrees in the car, so he didn't freeze to death. Oxygen levels in the car were good, so detectives knew he didn't suffocate. There was no evidence of a physical reason for his death. Experts later realized that he had mentally convinced himself that he was going to die. His mind was his cause of death.

Mind Expert Trevor Moawad said this: "As people, what we do is observe and report." I can't make a shot; my boss doesn't care about me; I'm having a bad day. Your thoughts dictate your physical and mental reactions to that observation. Therefore, your thoughts lead to your actions.

Negativity is the most dominant enemy we combat. Perspective, visualization, and mindset are so powerful they directly impact our ability to live. I won't survive; I can't do it; this is too hard. If you don't want to complete something, the first thing you say is, "I can't." These words communicate to the body, "shutdown". We must remove this combination of words from our vocabulary when facing character-refining moments.

You are what you tell yourself. We must learn to press the ESCAPE button and shut down the program our mind has been perpetuating. *Exit* the program. *Send* a higher intention to your mind. *Cancel* the limiting thought(s). *Access* healthy energy. *Program* a better thought pattern. *Envision* your desires.

The power of positive thought can bring your desires into reality! When you think constructively, you visualize powerfully, you prepare effectively, and you receive great results.

Thoughts---> **Actions** ---> **Results**. Train your mind and it will be your most powerful tool.

Negativity is just as powerful as positivity. Choose your mindset wisely knowing it will affect everything around you.

ACT: The No Complaining Rule

SHUT UP! Eliminate complaining and negative perspectives.

In 1991, Michael Jordan and the Chicago Bulls implemented a no complaining rule. They vowed not to complain about the conditions, referees, or their opponents. I don't think it was a coincidence that everyone developed physically and mentally because their only focus became what they could control. Oh, and that's also the year the Chicago Bulls won their first championship! Eliminating complaining and negative perspectives created ownership, toughness, and focus.

Letting go of the habit of complaining requires intentional practice. Omit toxic words and phrases to remove toxic energy. Remove them from your vocabulary and this will change your way of thinking. Challenge people around you to do the same sharing the conscious and subconscious effects.

It is not just your words that limit success. The feelings that are created by those pessimistic thoughts can block your progress. Fear and doubt are the #1 and #2 reasons people do not accomplish their dreams. Most people don't even make an attempt, so their potential, passion, and purpose are never properly introduced to the world.

The most beautiful gifts lie just on the other side of fear—growth, triumph, and love just to name a few. For 20+ years I had a fear of heights, also known as "a fear of what might happen." I randomly decided to jump out of a plane. I paid my skydiving deposit in advance because I hate wasting money and knew it would prevent me from backing out.

"What if I fall," my fears said. "What if I fly," my destiny interjected. I jumped. I fell fast—120 miles an hour—a 60-second freefall to be exact. But right on time my parachute ejected (Thank God), and I witnessed a vista I want you and everyone I know to see, a view of the beautiful things hidden behind fear. I saw my dreams.

Jumping from 15,000 feet was one of the best decisions I ever made. Since then, what was once my fear has taken me all over the world to see some of the most magnificent views, shifted my mindset, and given me a better sense of purpose. My life continues to blossom. Remember, the fears we don't face become our life's limitations. We must conquer our fears and doubts.

That is not to say that fear does not exist. If you truly care, fear is near. The most common fear in the world is that of public speaking. I am a professional speaker. My only desire is to reach those I am blessed to serve, and that brings about anxiety because I care deeply. You can't have courage without fear. Having a champion's mindset does not mean being fearless and not having human moments. It means leaning into those fears and thriving regardless because you have uncommon control over your thoughts.

1. Change Your State

> How you control your thoughts begins with your model of the world. What is your perspective? You cannot hold your past against your future.

We must convert our pain into strength and wisdom.

As mentioned in chapter three, your pain is an opportunity to rise or run. To rise, you must change your state. A champion's mentality acknowledges that pain is just another obstacle, another opportunity to show off your greatness. When Kobe Bryant tore his Achilles' in a 2013 game against the Golden State Warriors, before refusing to be carried off the court, he knocked down two big free throws to keep his team in the game. Then he walked off the court with his head held high, bearing a fully torn tendon in his foot. As he was being examined by trainers and other professionals, his family came into the training room. They were upset because he was visibly in pain. He told them that this was just another hurdle. He refused to let it define him or to cause him to leave the game he loved so much. That's one of many times that Kobe chose greatness. He decided to rise!

2. Mental Training

You must train your mind like athletes train their bodies. You want to mentally prepare yourself for the biggest challenges because the mind governs your actions, and your actions are the best control you can have over your results. This is why I choose to abstain from coffee, smoking, and other substances that people can become mentally dependent on. We must have the ability to control our own mental state. Can you make it through your day efficiently and effectively without your morning cup of fresh Folgers? It's the principle. The battle is won mentally well before it is won physically.

As you mentally train, remember that you are your biggest competition. It is not those ahead of you or beside you. When I think of this concept, I see the famous photo of Olympic Gold Medalist Michael Phelps with his eyes on the finish line. He had tunnel vision much like a horse with blinders on. The guy in the lane next to him had his eyes fixed on Michael. It appeared that to him beating Michael would represent success while for Michael victory came from being his best.

Michael Phelps is the best swimmer anyone in our lifetimes has ever seen. His mindset is to focus on the things that he can control: his personal preparation and performance. This is the approach we must have as we aspire to provide champion level value to the teams and organizations we are a part of.

To be a champion, you must have uncommon control, uncommon standards, and uncommon habits. You must live in a way that demands an explanation.

---

3. Confidence

Statistics reveal 85% of children and adults experience lack of confidence, self-doubt, or low self-esteem at some point in their lives. Whether during childhood or as an adult, struggles with confidence can be soul destroying. If we don't conquer our mind, our mind will surely conquer us. The good news is that we can overcome these mental hurdles.

Confidence is linked to nearly every element in life. It is what you think of yourself and your abilities. Those individuals who have overcome their challenges with low self-esteem steer towards success. Each of us is responsible for our thoughts. Life's tests present an opportunity for us to analyze our thinking and re-set strategies to ensure that we remain sure of ourselves and that we share positive thinking with our sphere of influence.

The trick is learning to overcome negative thinking. Some manage this while others do not. Instead, they carry around debilitating thoughts about their own self-worth for the rest of their lives, often revealed through addictive and negative habits. A few examples of this crippling mental state are settling for mediocrity by not performing at the level you are capable of, being highly critical of yourself, not believing you are deserving of success, and even exhibiting unhealthy addictions. Many believe that confidence can be taken by an event, a negative coach or boss, a parent or spouse. On the contrary, true confidence can't be taken, but it can be given.

Think of your favorite subject in school past or present. Who taught that class? Imagine this scenario: You are walking into the classroom. Your teacher is standing at the door and warmly greets you as you walk in. She or he says, "Good morning. Are you ready for our exam today?" Your jaw drops! You attempt to make it less obvious, but this exam totally slipped your mind. You were overwhelmed with so much this week.

You get to your desk and your heartbeat picks up. The lyrics of an old Eminem hit, "Lose Yourself," about sweaty palms and nervousness comes to mind. Like the lyrics mention, you may appear calm on the outside, but you're nervous on the inside. Then your mind is silenced by the slap of the test packet as it's dropped on your desk.

How do you feel right now? Words that cross your mind are probably anxious, unprepared, and not confident. You shamefully bomb that exam and rightfully so. Three weeks later another exam is scheduled. You put it on your calendar. You study thoroughly and even complete the study guide. As you walk into the classroom, you are greeted warmly as usual. Your teacher asks, "Good morning; are you prepared for our exam today?" You smile and without hesitation you respond, "Yes, I am!" as the melody of "Eye of the Tiger" creeps into your head. How do you feel as this visualization runs through your mind? You probably feel unstoppable, prepped, and confident and rightfully so.

Confidence comes from two things: how you prepare and what you think about daily. No one else can take these two things from you, but you can surely give them away. The only way that I can be confident about flying a plane is if I have studied and have had challenging and successful experiences flying a plane. This applies in all industries. Kobe said he was confident taking the last shot because he prepared himself daily to make that basket when the game was on the line. He created game-like pressure in practice, he trained at the highest level daily, and he visualized himself hitting big shots consistently. He was not concerned with approval. If you live for recognition, you will die from criticism. A key to champion level production is mindset. Confidence is earned. It can be given but not taken.

It is not simply skill that separates the good from the great. More importantly, the great ones have an unshakable confidence in their abilities because they see themselves succeeding.

Daily Practice: Mental Training

1. Use the ESCAPE technique.
2. Employ the No Complaining Rule.
3. Remember, you are your only competition.
4. Become your own biggest fan.
5. Remove negative words from your vocabulary.

B. Approach

1. Circle of Success

A talented group of young men from Michigan Men's Basketball Program of the early '90s and a popular phone company in the early 2000s referred to their top five as the Fab 5. Your own Fab 5 are the fabulous five people you connect with most often. Some of the most prominent research in the world proves that you will become the average of your Fab 5 financially, habitually, and mentally. Because you are around them so often, you will subconsciously pick up spending, eating, mentality, and other habits both good and bad. This is why millionaires tend to affiliate themselves with other millionaires and complainers find themselves around other complainers.

Your network is your net worth. It is no coincidence that Bill Gates and Warren Buffet are known besties. They're two bigtime influencers in their own respected spaces with the pocketbook to prove it. If you are around more positive, intrinsically motivated people, there is a greater chance that you will be influenced both consciously and subconsciously to be the same. "Show me your friends and I will show you your future." I heard that saying often as a child. You are also the books you read, the movies you watch, the music you listen to, and the conversations you engage in. When you alter things around you, things will begin to change inside of you.

Often success means rearranging our Fab 5. For those who are reading this who have not yet discovered your vision, you probably do not know what kind of circle of success to pursue. That's okay. You are reading the right book. Sometimes you have to first know who you are not to discover who you are. Rid yourself of the people in your life who encourage habits that you know will not propel you to whatever purpose is anxiously awaiting you. As you filter out contaminators, you will begin to find yourself among more like-minded, goal-oriented, purpose-driven contributors. Think quality over quantity.

When asked about his accomplishments in the film industry, Kobe Bryant credited his success to being surrounded by other obsessives like himself. He shared openly that he was not looking for things that he could do easily as the leader of a studio. He and his team were searching for the projects they weren't sure they could create, and they attacked the ones they chose optimistically. Kobe was always looking for a challenge. He needed people who thought just as outlandishly as he did. In return, through that mindset, they were able to reach a level that most didn't think was even possible, winning an Emmy and an Oscar.

Change your approach and elevate your standards and you will also raise the bar for those around you. The influence of excellence in your circle must be reciprocated.

2. Feed Your Focus

Be Hungry. The last place you want to be is between a lion and his meal. These beasts act as if they need it, they deserve it, and they will do anything necessary to get it. I have a true appreciation for wild animals, so *Animal Planet*, *National Geographic* and *Our Planet* on Netflix keep me amazed. The way a lion stalks its prey is how we should pursue our aspirations—with an acute awareness but still an innate ability to starve our distractions and feed our focus.

This locked in, confident mindset secured through undeniable preparation is champion mentality. Your mindset is what you must control to get the results you seek. Narrow your focus, which requires sacrifice. If you don't sacrifice for what you want, then ultimately what you want becomes the sacrifice. To elevate your success, you must forfeit your lesser desires for your greater ones.

Excuses and results cannot be mentioned in the same conversation. One contradicts the other.

ACT: List of Affirmations

Remind yourself often of the qualities you possess that make you special. Complete your list of five as a common practice. Feel free to come up with more than five. This is great for controlling energy flow, narrowing your focus, and sharpening your confidence. Be honest about what you think of yourself and remain positive. If you find yourself struggling with this, it's an exercise you should consider doing daily.

Examples:

- *I am a contributor. I am not intimidated by what I do not know but encouraged by the insight I can provide.*

- *I am a great shooter because of my intentional daily preparation and my ability to control my thoughts in clutch situations.*

- *I am an impactful leader, selfless in my actions and interactions.*

C. Performance

In his first season as a Laker, Kobe Bryant airballed four shots in the final five minutes of a playoff game. The media scrutinized his performance, calling him overrated, an NBA bust, and everything else but a son of God. He, along with the rest of the Lakers team, arrived back in Los Angeles in the wee hours of the morning following the game. Everyone else rushed home, but the rookie left the airport after their chartered flight and drove to Palisades High School near where he lived. His friend, the school janitor, let him into the gym, where he shot until sunup. He trained to make the shots that his opponent made tough for him. At this high school, he imagined being on a stage as high as the one he had just performed on hours earlier. This was probably the most important and defining moment in Kobe's career because, after airballing the first and second shots, most players wouldn't even have attempted a third. Even after falling short, it was like he told himself, "You can't make a shot you don't take. You have earned this opportunity."

They say that after falling off of a horse you have to get back on right away before allowing fear and discouragement to grow. The same is true when it comes to career performance of any kind. That's why Kobe went to the gym to practice those shots all night. He was willing to keep shooting in the face of that well publicized, less than stellar playoff loss and later became one of the best shooting guards the game has seen. A champion's performance demands perseverance through preparation. It does not require perfection, but it does demand consistency.

A champion's mindset is not driven by results. It is driven by their distinct desire to master the process.

Key Questions:

1. Where does your confidence come from?

2. Why is it important to control your thoughts?

3. What are two mental training habits you will practice daily?

4. How can you respond in an uncommon way during character refining moments?

CHAMPIONS' Code: We must have an innate ability to concentrate on our training and outperform ourselves daily. Your focus today must be to train or perform at a level higher than you did yesterday. Champions don't compete with others; they compete with self. Strive for self-discipline, execution, and personal records. It's okay to be your biggest critic, but, most importantly, champions are their own biggest fans.

5
PREPARATION
THE PURSUIT OF EXCELLENCE

Every living human being on this planet has access to the exact same amount of time in each day. Each morning, all of us are credited 86,400 seconds, which is equivalent to 24 hours. Each night when the clock strikes 12, the time we failed to maximize is discarded. There are no refunds. There are no advances. With each day comes a new 86, 400 seconds. This philosophy was first introduced by French Novelist Marc Levy. Today is a gift, so you must live in the present. Take full advantage of your investment of time to maximize your potential. Your clock is ticking. How will you make the most of today?

Action Creates Transformation.

Salary.com conducted a study that found that the average person wastes nearly two hours each day. This is not the time you spend recovering from a workout or paying attention to your family. These are two hours of unintentional nothingness, and that adds up to 14 wasted hours a week. How much more could we accomplish and who would we become if we had 56 more intentional hours every month or even just a fraction of that amount of time?

Our actions directly impact our destiny. Whether you want to become an investor or a chef or to win a championship, everything you seek to accomplish in life requires an intentional investment of time better known as preparation. There is no substitute. In our pursuit of excellence, we will unpack the four Ps that define a champion's preparation: Purpose, Promise, Process, Pursuit.

Purpose

Why? That's one of the first questions toddlers learn to value. Why this and why that? They want to know how the world around them works. My question to you is, why? Why are you reading this book? Why are you alive? Why are you on this journey? If your vision is huge, and it should be, you can trust that there will be obstacles just as big. You must keep your *why* in the forefront of your mind to remain focused and humble and to have clarity of direction. Your purpose is the compass for your vision.

Purpose is found at the intersection of your talents, impact, and passion. This includes what you are good at, the service you provide, and what you love. It is not directly tied to wealth or popularity though that may come. Your purpose is bigger than any of that. Know the value of your purpose and pursue it relentlessly. Don't get stuck fulfilling someone else's dream and forget your own. Someone somewhere is depending on you to do what you are called to do. Stop playing it safe. Fulfill your purpose so that those in your life now and those who will come after you will be able to find the guidance they need to elevate their success. This alone makes your vision bigger than you.

Protect your purpose. Not everyone deserves an explanation of or an opinion about your dreams. It is senseless to request directions from people who have never been where you are going. Choose a Fab 5 that will provide truth, which is always important, but also a tribe that will fan your fire. Time will always be a challenge. It is one of the most squandered of all personal resources. If you are not purposeful about choosing those with whom you spend your time, then you will leave your results to chance.

Before growth comes challenge to prepare you for your purpose.

Promise

I have heard it said too many times: "The greatest predictor of the future is your past." False! The greatest predictor of the future is not your past. Your daily practices define your future. This is why there are so many success stories of homeless people becoming outstanding influencers and millionaires like Jim Carey and players who were cut from their high school teams who become arguably the greatest of all time like Michael Jordan.

It begins with your vision and a daily promise to yourself. It's not about righting your wrongs; it's about committing to the present and writing the future you desire. Make a daily pledge to yourself that you are going to *show up* to become your best self as a leader, teammate, co-worker, sibling, parent, spouse, friend, etc. You want to train and ingrain the habits needed to excel. A habit is something you have done so many times that your body outperforms your mind. Similar to breathing, you can do it without thought, simply on instinct. Your commitment to your habits is your roadmap to the championship level. The daily practice that you commit to will build your character as an individual, also adding value to the world we live in.

Commitment is needed to achieve breakthrough results. What happens when you don't feel like it? If you only went to work, class, or practice on the days you felt like it, you may as well not go at all. Will you choose to quit or to survive? Or will you be reminded of who you are committed to being and choose to thrive? Decide now who you are in defining moments—before the loss, before you are denied, before the heartbreak, before the setbacks. Choose your identity now! It will be much easier to find yourself in the midst of turmoil when you are already familiar with the person you have chosen to be. Otherwise, you will revert to what comes easily or naturally. Procrastination, distractions, and lack of readiness are just a few of the hurdles that may get it in way. This may mean starting with the habits you must avoid. As mentioned previously, sometimes to find out who you are, you must first discover who you are not.

Stop should'n on yourself and make the commitment
that activates your greatness.

Process

"Rome wasn't built in a day," the saying goes. Known for its unparalleled architecture and historic monuments, Rome is home to some of the most iconic buildings ever built. This adage, which originated in France, is a reminder of the patience needed to develop anything grand. The ancient architects of this beautiful city measured each brick inch by inch and laid each by hand, one at a time. With great vision, precision, intentionality, and commitment to the process, they cut no corners. Their uncommon attention to detail created what we now know as the Eternal City.

No, Rome was not built in one day. In fact, like each of us, it is still a constant work in progress. It has taken nearly 2,800 years of intense labor, unexpected challenges, and refining moments—an essential process.

Trust the process. This mantra is both practical and spiritual as I sum up all of my experiences in life. I heard those words from many mentors, coaches, and supervisors. "Yes, okay, Coach," I said countless times, often masking my sarcastic response. You also may have heard this phrase and, like me, labeled it as an excuse for not getting something you felt you deserved. I wanted to be a starter during my sophomore year at Northern Illinois University, and, if you asked me, I deserved to be. At the point in the season when I realized it, stats validated my argument. I led our team in multiple statistical categories. I've always been told, "Women lie, men lie, but numbers don't!" I was on a quest to prove myself in practice every day. I eventually worked up the nerve to approach my Position Coach E.C. Hill.

"Coach, I don't want to sound selfish," I said, "but I have a question to ask you. Why am I not in the starting lineup?"

She looked from across her desk and sat back in her seat. She responded, "Marke, you finish every close game, you are top three in minutes played, and you're concerned about a three-second tip?"

Everyone puts value on starting, right? The best of the best start the game, don't they? These were my thoughts. I was so wrong. I tied my personal success to position and title and not productivity or value. I wasn't thinking about the success of the team, which definitely made my thoughts selfish.

In time I came to realize that this is the mindset of the average. Later that year I received 6th (Wo)Man of the Year honors in the Mid-American Conference. I accepted my award at our conference tournament in front of every player, coach, and administrator from each team in the MAC.

After receiving the award and heading back to my seat, Coach E.C. stopped me and said, "This is just the beginning." I didn't fully understand. She continued, "You are important to this team, and the role you have been given is the role we need from you. Star in it and trust the process."

This became a daily conversation. "The process is taking the necessary steps to become the player you want to be in the time necessary. You embrace it by working your butt off to improve and helping others improve in practice. By starring in your role and showing up to do your job as well as it can be done consistently." Coach E.C. told me, "If you continue to trust the process, you have the potential to be an all-conference player every year for the remainder of your career."

That was one of my many moments of revelation. I shifted my mindset from rank and status to preparation and process. My focus changed and so did my results. Because of my preparation, I improved my production, and because of my production I earned all-conference and all-league honors for the remainder of my college and professional playing career.

The results do not come before the effort. The process is where success happens and transformation is made. The results are just the evidence of the greatness that took place during the process. Like baking a cake, if not for the process, you wouldn't get the results you seek. If you bypass or avoid one step in your life, the cake your taste buds anticipated will be disappointing. Each ingredient is important. You cannot skip a step. There is no substitute for time. The process is what it takes!

Preparation for athletes includes film study, training, and visualization. For professionals, it may require organization, research, and development. Truly preparing means doing extra, not just enough, not cutting corners but instead going the extra inch. Quality, not quantity.

Success doesn't come based on the number of hours you put in but rather from intentional work. You don't commit to that kind of meaningful work in order to receive some kind of acknowledgment but rather to champion your skills. If you cannot make strides towards your goal in the 86,400 seconds you are given each day, it's not a goal; it's a dream. If all you have are dreams, sleep is the only place you will find them.

Your character is defined by what you do most often. Excellence therefore is a way of life, not a single act.

Pursuit

Warren Buffett has an $78.9 billion net worth, making him the seventh-wealthiest person in the world. He prides his success on his pursuit to become one of the best in the field of investment. He has accomplished that and maintained his success for some time now. In an HBO documentary on his life, Buffet, who spends between five and six hours a day thumbing through books and newspapers, says he enjoys thinking about investment problems and business concerns. He reminds viewers that everyone has access to the same materials that inform his decisions, so anyone can make the effort and rise to the occasion. He has simply outstudied all of his opponents while relentlessly pursuing his passion for investing. He has learned everything that he possibly could about his craft, eventually gaining so much of an advantage that he seems impossible to catch. While others are competing against Buffet, he is competing against himself.

The quest to become a champion requires an unrelenting pursuit of excellence. Your desire must be undeniable and your effort must be unmatched. Do not allow anything to force you to lose sight of your vision. If it's not your number one priority, it's a distraction. Your work ethic must be unmeasurable, but don't mistake activity with productivity. Work hard and smart with an uncommon intentionality and a drive of rare comparison. The quest for excellence is inspirational. Follow your vision to such an extent that you elevate the productivity of those around you. Chase your dreams.

"No" does not always mean "no." It often means "not right now" or "not this way." If you can't get in through the front door, try the back door, then the side door.

Raise the bar. You cannot rise to low standards. A champion's expectations must remain extremely high. There are no shortcuts when seeking championship level success. It requires a studious approach. Study the minds and journeys of respected leaders in your industry. Research and apply what you learn. Choose to be the dumbest person in the room in order to absorb as much knowledge and expertise as you can. Find mentors and peers who are credible and like-minded. Your circle of success is not based on quantity; it's determined by quality. Surround yourself with people who are headed in the same direction.

Even Warren Buffet will tell you there is no secret formula. Long term success is earned. Don't run from the work!

Daily Practice: The 4 Ps Daily Routine

There are four things you must practice daily to discover your inner champion.

- Purpose – Keep your *why* in the forefront!
- Promise – Commit to be your best self.
- Process – Embrace life's challenges.
- Pursuit – Relentlessly pursue excellence!

ACT: Vision Commitment

Step 1: Begin by writing a vow to who you are committed to being, explaining the actions you will apply to become the version of yourself that you envision. Your commitment is not specific or limited to your career. How you show up as a friend, significant other, parent, influencer, neighbor, and stranger are also important.

We all have strengths and opportunities and our commitment should speak to both. We need to be intentional about not calling them weaknesses but *opportunities* because they are chances for growth. Write your opportunities as if they are already strengths. Think about the habits needed to make your opportunities a strength and apply those practices. That should be where you direct your focus. As discussed in chapter 4, avoid negative language. The words you speak have power. Use expressions of empowerment and affirmation.

Review your Vision Commitment daily as a reminder of how you will show up. Recite it like you believe it has already come to fruition. *ACT* like you know it! (ACT means Action Creates Transformation.) Place your Commitment Vision in numerous locations so you see it often. Write it in your notebook, put it on the screensaver of your phone and/or the desktop of your computer, type it up and frame it. It can serve as your written vision board. There is no limit to how long or how short it should be. Your Vision Commitment is always evolving much like you as a person. As an opportunity becomes a strength, find other areas of your life that require intentionality and add them to your vow.

Step 2: Find an accountability partner. Remember not just anyone deserves this role. Your accountability partner must be someone who will give you truth over harmony. They will tell you what you need to hear and not just what you want to hear. They will be someone who will encourage you to be the version of yourself you are committed to being and not allow you to do things that are detrimental to your success. Choose a person you speak to regularly whom you trust with your dreams, fears, strengths, and flaws. Your accountability partner is the person who helps you make your vision a reality.

Step 3: Pursue mentorship: It's hard to improve when you have no one else but yourself to follow. Iron sharpens iron. A common misconception is that you have to be a certain age to have a mentor. This couldn't be further from the truth. In fact, I would say the sooner the better. You can have a mentor at 10 or at 80 years of age. You are not too young nor too old. The moment we stop seeking development, we halt growth. A mentor is a person who has accomplished something you are working to achieve. This person must also share a similar "why" and "way" of doing what you are most passionate about. This individual will serve as your Morpheus to Neo, Muffet McGraw to Niele Ivy, or Mr. Miyagi to the Karate Kid.

They will provide the blueprint, accountability, and wisdom needed to prepare you for and guide you through the process.

Remember, it is up to you to become a champion. As the old saying goes, a horse can be led to water, but you cannot make him drink. This book invites you to take command of your life, but only you can decide to *act*!

Another common mistaken belief is that you can only have one mentor. This is false. You can have a variety of mentors who serve in different areas of your life. Just as you go to your podiatrist when you are having foot issues, to your ophthalmologist for your eye checkups, and to the body shop to get your bumper replaced, you have mentors who specialize in different areas. I personally have spiritual, professional, financial, and relational mentors. I'm fortunate to have people who can cover multiple bases, but each of them specializes in one area of my life. They can speak to the success and challenges I have and will experience. These amazing beings have helped me continue to evolve into the woman I aspire to be. Your mentors can provide the same value.

Key Questions: Student's Mindset

To be a master of your craft, you must also be a student. Study and apply the journeys and habits of greats inside and outside of your field who have become world-class champions. Model their success. Find someone who has shared your experiences and achieved your goals. Study them, follow them, watch them! Research and ask questions.

1. How can they be defined?
2. What makes them who they are?
3. What sets them apart?
4. What resources have they provided?
5. What do they have that I am missing?

CHAMPIONS' Code: You show you care by how you prepare—by being efficient and effective in all the ways you strive to fulfill your purpose and achieve the dreams you seek and by preparing with a student's approach and a surgeon's precision. Champions do not mistake activity for productivity. We are deliberate with each action because of our commitment to our better selves. Champions respect the process and practice patience, understanding that the dream is free but the hustle is sold separately. Our pursuit is incomparable and undeniable.

6

INFLUENCE

THE GREATEST SUPERPOWER IN THE WORLD

Influence is the greatest superpower any human being can possess. It's the innate ability to guide a person or group. If you have the power to influence, you have the ability to impact the world, which conveniently includes your business and/or team. An unknown secret is that everyone has the aptitude to lead because everyone has the ability to influence. With this superpower comes great responsibility. It's not about being in charge. It's a commitment to the elevation of others.

Our world has featured a number of powerful leaders, some of those positive and others who use their ability to influence with unethical intentions to inflict harm, exclude others, or selfishly to elevate their own success.

Some even have caused wars and destroyed entire countries. Whether good or bad as leaders, each is extremely effective. As was often depicted in our childhood cartoons, it is our hope that this superpower does not get in the hands of the wrong person. The champion's creed is a commitment to handle this great power with care

The Power of Influence

You are in the checkout line at the grocery store. Each queue seems to stretch as far as your eyes can see. People around you are growing impatient. From your spot in line, you scan the store and notice that the counter in sporting goods is open. You grab your cart and make the move. The cashier greets you and begins helping you unload your cart. You are relieved. As you look over your shoulder, you notice a lady with two children has jumped out of the same line to join you, and you greet them with a smile. Just behind her, two other shoppers see opportunity and join the movement. You are a trailblazer, initiating a change that enhanced the experience and potentially the lives of five other people. If each of those five people impact five others in a similar way, you directly and indirectly improved the lives of 30 people! Imagine how many lives you can impact in your lifetime. The power of influence is great both directly and indirectly. This emphasizes that leadership is an ongoing cycle. To continue to grow as a groundbreaker, every champion must understand and appreciate the five distinct levels of leadership.

Five Levels of Leadership

LEVEL 1: Follow – To be a special leader, you first have to be able to follow. You must know who to follow and when. This first step is the main downfall of influencers. Their pride gets in the way of the vision. This can be hazardous to the mission of the group. Great leaders have the gift of altruism. Regardless of title or rank, you must be willing to let go of self to assure the success of those around you.

LEVEL 2: Lead Self – To lead others, you must learn to lead yourself. You must model the behavior you want to see from your teammates and associates. This is one of the most important things you'll ever do as a leader. Most of us have witnessed a person who tried to tell others how to do their jobs while they were not so good at taking care of their own responsibilities. Credibility is a key ingredient in leadership. To earn the trust and respect of your co-workers, teammates, boss or coach, you must consistently show up, meeting and, even better, exceeding expectations when it comes to your own responsibilities. Be sure to look at yourself realistically so that you can understand where your personal difficulties come from and where your personal strengths are rooted.

LEVEL 3: Lead One Person – You cannot be a level three leader unless you have completed the pre-requisites. To be a leader of great influence, you must be able to follow and to lead yourself before you can guide anyone else. This also requires trust, which is created through authentic relationships established by knowing the "why" and the "way" of others. What motivates them? Understanding this allows you as a leader to support them in their best way and help elevate their performance.

LEVEL 4: Lead a Small Group – Level four leaders have a rare ability to zoom out and identify the needs of those around them while personally performing at a high level. They are inclusive, sure not to neglect the ultimate goal, and consistently expressive of the value of each person while influencing the direction of the group. To be this kind of leader, you must be an outstanding follower, leader of self, and leader of others individually.

LEVEL 5: Lead a Large Group – At this level, you will lead from the front of the charge. To attain this position, you must first master levels one through four. A good leader can influence others, but a special leader can *create* other leaders. This person has the capacity to elevate the success of the company or team all while supporting others and grooming new leaders.

Each level of leadership is equally as important. Each individual within the group must know his or her role and star within that role. If everyone embraces their part, the entire team will be operating at a championship level, which gives your organization the best chance of earning the results you seek.

Do not allow egotism to limit your success. True leadership is never being afraid to stray away from the ideas of the pack and also not being too prideful to stick with the group. This leadership system supports the idea that everyone is a leader, and the most powerful leadership module is leading down, leading across, and leading up within the hierarchy of a group. This concept starts first with each person's development, then equips each individual to lead from their respected positions ranging from level one to level five leadership.

To sustain substantial success, you must maintain magnanimous leadership.

Pillars of Leadership: Servanthood

When I think of the greatest leaders, those who come to mind are people like Gandhi, Mother Teresa, and Nelson Mandela, some of the most influential human beings in the world. They used their influence to encourage world peace, equality, and a number of other powerful movements. Their magnanimous leadership attracted the hearts and minds of millions around the globe. Their greatest gift was their servant's heart, not their power. They gave so much for the growth of others and the elevation of humanity. Servant leaders recognize that their vision is bigger than themselves.

Transformational over Transactional

Everything rises and falls on leadership: teams, companies, schools, churches, families, countries, etc.

If you know anything about Dennis Rodman, you know that he was is a unique specimen. He struggled with structure but he rarely struggled to perform. You should also know that he was one of the best rebounders and defensive players basketball has ever seen. He was a key part of the Chicago Bulls dynasty and the third musketeer of the Michael Jordan and Scottie Pippen trio. Every players role was just as different as their needs but each player was extremely valuable.

Phil Jackson, Bulls Head Coach, 13x NBA Champion met Rodman where he was. Jackson understood that he needed to give Rodman additional freedom to do things he enjoyed outside of basketball in order to get his best on the court. Most leaders are not willing to go an extra inch or mile to support those in their charge. The way Coach Jackson understood Rodman is a perfect example of knowing the personality of those we serve. This is one of the most prominent skills of exceptional leaders. There is no "one size fits all" way to approach leadership. The media attempted to make the player/coach relationship between Coach Jackson and Rodman difficult to manage. Incorrect. Coach Jackson knew and catered to Rodman's needs as a human before the player. Decisions are only hard to make when it is not clear what is most important. Each person within any organization has different needs. Transformational leadership is identifying that and being willing to support them in the way that is best fitting for the individual within your care.

Leaders, don't get so caught up in results that you forget to show others how to show up. Don't get so focused on telling people what to do that you forget to ask how they're doing. Don't become so fixated on speaking that you forget to listen. Don't forget: Leadership is service.

Transformational leadership can take place only when there is trust and respect. This can only happen if deposits are made. Think of an automated teller machine (ATM). The most common transactions that take place at an ATM are deposits and withdrawals. You cannot make a withdrawal from a debit account unless you have made prior deposits. The same rules apply in transformational leadership. We cannot demand of others unless we have served and equipped them. Leadership deposits come when we offer additional time, energy, and resources to those we serve. This includes celebrating privately and publicly to acknowledge each individual for his or her value.

Sounds like a lot, right? Very few embrace this responsibility, which is why only a small number in any industry have the ability to lead a team to the championship level. It's not what you do; it's how you do it. These deposits make those around us feel empowered and appreciated, which can increase their performance. Like good financial practices, you want to make far more deposits than you do withdrawals. This establishes credit and builds interest. It should never be a 1:1 ratio. The transformational leader consistently achieves great results because their deposits far outweigh their withdrawals.

In contrast, a transactional leader is someone who demands of others while offering few or no deposits, making withdrawal after withdrawal. These leaders frequently say, "I need this," or "Can you stay late?" They may inundate employees with emails at ungodly hours and on holidays. If you practice this kind of leadership, before long you may find yourself in the red because your withdrawals far outnumber your deposits, which will result in you losing the trust and respect of your team, counterparts, and spouse.

> "People don't care how much you know until they
> know how much you care." —Theodore Roosevelt

I have worked with a transactional leader. Just before I decided to part ways, I realized I had moved to a different state and neglected what I valued most to fully support my then boss, who wouldn't even tell me, "Good morning." There was no attempt to connect authentically, but I was expected to be accessible 24 hours a day. It was detrimental to my happiness, which made it easy to resign even when our results were at their best.

Your goal is not to be a boss who only orders people around. There is a big difference between a leader and a boss or dictator. The champion's creed is to transform the lives and experiences of everyone you are fortunate to serve as a leader. What you wish to experience, provide for others.

Our influence is based on how unselfishly we serve. If we constantly measure the pluses and minuses in our relationships, whether professional or personal, rather than acting as friends or team members, we become bookkeepers or scorekeepers. That's no way to honor a relationship. Fifty-fifty is a losing proposition. For some this may sound like a win, but it is not success. The only successful approach is giving one hundred percent. Make your win about the other person's needs. If there is a competition, it should be a race to do more, not a contest to see who can do the least and still receive a bigger return on their selfish investment. If both parties give one hundred percent, all expectations will be met or exceeded, and this will elevate the team and everyone within it.

What kind of leader are you? Review the following chart to identify your strengths and your opportunities.

Daily Practice:
Transformational vs. Transactional

Transformational Leadership	Transactional Leadership
Consistently deposits	Consistently withdraws
Impact driven	Result driven
Leads by example	Bossy
Relational	Irrational
Inclusive	Dismissive
Does more than expected	Fifty-fifty effort
Elevates	Manages
Accountable	Lacks humility
Challenges	Criticizes
Understanding	Inconsiderate
Accessible	Unapproachable
Willful listener	Quick to speak

Key Questions:

If any one of the transactional leadership qualities can be used to describe your leadership style even the least bit, you must be honest and note that it is an area deserving of immediate intentional development. Answer the questions below in your *CHAMPIONS' Creed Workbook*.

Once you have written down those specific areas that require growth, identify future opportunities to practice your new approach as a transformational leader as new opportunities present themselves. Lead with the main goal in mind, which is to serve. Allow your heart to guide you through each interaction.

1. What type of leader do you desire to be?

2. What are three areas mentioned in the chart above that require more of your attention as a transformational leader?

3. What are three specific ways that you will change your habits to better lead those in your charge?

The power of influence flows both ways. I can influence you and you can influence me just as greatly. Leadership, therefore, is a circular process.

Daily Practice: Connect 4

A question I receive from my clients often is how to create authentic relationships. Time is usually a challenge, considering the expectation of executing. Who really has time to form authentic professional relationships? The answer is simple. Champions make the time. But simple does not always mean easy. When you realize that this determines your company or team's success in profit and achievement, you will make time. I always share that leadership begins well before the game, event, work, and even long before practice. It starts before you even arrive at the office or gym.

What is the first thing we grab when we wake up? What is the last thing we take a look at before we go to sleep? Most would say their cell phones. A crucial part of being a champion is recognizing our habits that do not contribute to who we aspire to be and see them as opportunities.

Instead of thumbing through irrelevant tabloids and social media posts, how about using that time to Connect 4? Many of us are familiar with the board game. Connect 4 means to connect with four people. Reach out to the colleagues, teammates, and relatives that you don't speak with often, someone who may need to hear from you, someone you may be at odds with, or someone you speak to daily but you haven't connected with deeply. Take that time in the mornings or evening to tell four people how invaluable they are, offer your support, or just send a note saying that you are thinking of them. This is a great way to build trust and respect, which is needed to create authentic, culture changing relationships.

Leaders Leading Leaders

Level 5 leadership is the ability to create other leaders and high performers. It is your responsibility to build those around you.

The superpower of influence is empowering. A great example of this level of influence occurred in the 1997 NBA playoffs. Steve Kerr had missed shot after shot. Then, during a timeout near the end of the game, Michael Jordan, the best player in the world and his team leader, encouraged and supported him. Coming out of that huddle, Kerr then stepped up to make the shot that secured the 1997

NBA Title! This happened only after MJ had prepared him in practice, encouraged him, and empowered him in the moment. Transformational leadership enhances the human performance. This is greatest superpower any human being can have.

Those within our reach can only rise to the level of their leaders' expectations. Like plants, if well nourished, our team will outgrow their positions. We must continue to create environments that are conducive to growth. If you have lived up to your responsibilities as a leader, your assistant coaches will become sought after head coaches. You may have underclassmen who become Level 5 leaders. Your interns may become associates and eventual CEOs. This is the reason Google is one of the most pursued businesses to work for. The tech titan receives roughly three million job applications annually because of their luxe employee perks and ability to consistently position their employees to elevate.

Be the leader you wish you had.

Lead by Example

"You lead from the front!" That's one of my favorite quotes from one of my favorite childhood movies, *Love & Basketball*. In the film, Freshman Point Guard Monica Wright hoped to earn a starting role on her college team, but, during conditioning and practice, she constantly found herself in the middle of the pack, which is not the place for a champion. Her coach gave her truth over harmony that would eventually get her a starting position and win the team a national championship. "You lead from the front" in your presence, preparation, and performance. Championship leaders are always setting the bar higher.

Leadership is a lifestyle. There is a certain way that you must show up consistently. You are liable for the life and the growth of another human being. There is no greater responsibility. If the only time you lead is when you are winning or when you personally are performing well, you are a poor leader. Leadership is sometimes inconvenient. During such times, direction is most needed. Champions lead when they don't feel like it, when they are not being acknowledged, and do what is right even when their personal numbers dwindle and they are being ridiculed. As a champion, your words, actions, and energy must all align.

In the spring of 2016, I had the great pleasure of visiting Notre Dame women's basketball team just before they were due to take off for the ACC Tournament. During my time on campus, I observed a women's basketball practice and had a chance to connect with legendary Coach Muffet McGraw, an outstanding leader. I was wise enough to have a series of questions prepared just in case we found some time to chat and I'm happy I did. One comment I made during our discussion sparked an unforgettable conversation.

I mentioned, "You have an all-women's staff; this little girl from Springfield, Illinois, needed to see this. I've played on probably a dozen teams and had very few female coaches."

Coach McGraw turned to me and said, "That is exactly why. Young girls need to see leaders who look like them."

In a press conference during the 2019 Final Four, she shared a powerful speech that shook the sports world. She advocated for passing the Equal Rights Amendment, which is intended to prohibit sex discrimination and guarantee equal rights for women. Although the amendment was introduced over 50 years ago, it still hasn't passed. She boldly stated that female head coaches should be a norm and not an exception. Since Title IX, the number of female coaches has dwindled limiting the number of visible female leaders. It is important for young women to have someone who looks like them in positions of power, helping them prepare for their future—not only because they are female but because there are more than enough who are qualified to coach the game at the highest level and teach essential life skills. These opportunities should be the same in corporate America where less than 5% of CEOs in Fortune 500 companies are women. This was a powerful statement made by a phenomenal woman who leads from in front of the charge, one who has chosen to lead the right way and in times of challenge and inconvenience.

As influencers, it is our God-given responsibility to show up daily, speak up often, and stand out always.

I jump on opportunities to be the least smart person in

the room. I was fortunate to be in a small group that was invited to sit down with Dr. Condoleezza Rice in April of 2019. There were six words she shared that truly changed my life: "Someone has to be the first."

Condoleezza Rice is the first woman and first African American to serve as provost of Stanford University. In 2001, she was appointed National Security Adviser, becoming the first African American (and woman) to hold the post, and went on to become the first black woman to serve as U.S. Secretary of State. She shared with me that her goal was not to be the first; it was to be great, but to be great, you often have to be the first. She later realized the honor that comes with leading the charge. She was a trailblazer.

The champion's creed is a commitment to paving the way for many who will come after you. Whether you are the first graduate of your family, a first-generation immigrant, or the first minority politician in your city, recognize you have the power to set and raise the bar.

The time for transformational leadership is now. Lead from where you are with the intent to elevate and empower. This power does not come without great responsibility, servanthood, selflessness, and transformation. As you shift your actions to become a true leader, you transform the lives of those in your reach and those you serve as a trailblazer.

ACT: In Memory of…

Many of us are familiar with an obituary. It is an informational program summarizing the life of an individual following his or her death. I have attended my share of funeral services. I have learned that funeral attendees share a series of stories and memories. It is easy to get an idea of the type of person who has transitioned.

Your task now is to create your own obituary, answering a series of questions. When I first completed this exercise, it changed my life. It exposed blind spots I didn't realize I had as a leader, blind spots I could not wait to get rid of. It helped me better understand what I value and the legacy I want to leave. This exercise can be every bit as impactful for you if you give it the required time, transparency, and vulnerability. The more of this you allow, the more transformational this practice can be for you, your family, your relationships, your career, and your clarity of purpose.

A goal in life should be for us to live in such a way that those around us do not have to make up cheerful stories about the type of person we were while we were alive. My intent in giving this assignment is not to be morbid or trigger paranoia but instead to help you get well below the surface and to the heart. If you were to pass suddenly, at this very moment, what would others say about your character and your service as a leader? Fill in the blanks below. This assignment begins with honesty first. If you find this a difficult exercise, embrace the challenge and recognize the areas of opportunity in front of you. Remember truth over harmony for transformational results.

On this day, we celebrate the memorable life of
_____. _____
was known   most   for _____.
_____ consistently brought _____, _____,
and_____, to our workplace and our lives.
_____ was also a great _____ who
really _____ _____. _____
_____ is irreplaceable and is something
that will live through everyone _____ has touched
forever.

The truth is that none of us know the day or the hour that our lives in the flesh will end. How will you leave others? What will be your legacy? Is the world better because you existed? The beautiful thing is that you are still alive and you have a chance to make an instant impact on those around you. Review your obituary and answer these key questions.

Key Questions:

1. What lasting impact do I want to have on others from this day forward?

2. What are three qualities or habits I must implement to make this transformation a daily practice?

3. When will I begin?

CHAMPIONS' Code: The vision, this team, this position is bigger than me. As champions, we let go of ourselves to assure the success of those around us. We lead by example, not for self but for everyone. Champions leave those we come in contact with better than they were before we met them. Our approach and goal is not to fix but to give and live with a heart that seeks to serve and elevate.

7

OWNERSHIP
THE LAWS OF ACCOUNTABILITY

Blame is a prey's mental shackles. It is the inability to see one's own responsibility in certain situations. When I can blame it on my staff, I don't have to think about the areas where I failed them as a leader. When I can blame a game on the referees, I don't have to consider my poor decisions as a player or my lack of adjustments as a coach. When you seek to blame, you don't have to reflect on the areas where you need to improve. Blame is hazardous to the development of any individual or group. Refusing to take ownership will stunt your growth.

The Laws of Accountability

Blame has a conflicting affiliation with ownership. There is an old saying: when you point one finger at someone else, there are three fingers pointing back at you. Accountability is taking ownership of your life like a lion owns the jungle. A lion doesn't blame the jungle when he falls from a tree or when his prey eludes him. We must take responsibility for our actions, reactions, responses, and re-percussions.

Most people are willing to take responsibility for the good but want to deflect the bad. It takes a special someone to own his or her part when things are not ideal at work, at school, at home, and anywhere in between. Accountability is a life stance. Yes, being answerable for your circumstances can be difficult but not as hard as spending your life running from them. Choose your hard. It requires vulnerability, which is scary but not nearly as frightening as giving up. Choose your scary. It takes strength and self-awareness. You must be able to self-reflect and correct, knowing that ultimately, by choosing your actions, you also create your results. Making the decision to accept responsibility also requires vulnerability, which is the bridge from your flaws to your destiny and from your current reality to your dreams. To get to where you want to be, you must be honest about where you came from and where you are now. It is all connected.

Star in Your Role

Develop the habit of setting standards that others will be measured by. This will make you invaluable to any company or team you choose to affiliate yourself with.

Andre Iguodala and I grew up in the same town, Springfield, Illinois. From high school to college and college to the NBA, I watched him dominate within his role. On some teams his job was scoring, and on others he defended and led. Regardless of his role, he played it to the best of his abilities.

I traveled to the Bay to catch him in action. We caught up after the game. I congratulated him on the win and jokingly said, "You didn't look bad out there for year 12."

His performance was nothing short of outstanding as the numbers revealed. He responded saying, "I just try to do all the little things well and whatever my team needs from me." These words were spoken with great humility, but his actions supported his every word.

Now 16 years into his NBA career, he is a three-time NBA Champion, two-time Gold Medalist, Finals MVP, two-time NBA All-Defensive Team, NBA All-Star, and the list goes on. Warriors Head Coach Steve Kerr mentioned him during a playoff press conference, explaining that he knew he could count on Andre to perform at both ends of the court and felt more relaxed having him in the game.

Champions find value in their roles regardless of the size of the part they play. They own their responsibilities and star in them consistently.

In an orchestra, each instrument is equally important. If the violinist is off by one key, it can disrupt the entire production. If the percussionist is off beat, it ruins the entire piece. Each musician, associate, player, and leader must star in his or her role to contribute to the overall production of the group.

Control the Controllable

Keep your goals high and your standards higher. You cannot rise to low standards. Excuses are designed to avoid personal accountability. Personal responsibility is intended to limit limitations. You've probably heard the saying that you cannot have both excuses and results. Champions believe that there are no excuses good enough to keep them from accomplishing their goals. Yes, there will be obstacles. Things you cannot control, like other people, unfairness, etc. Champions remain true to the code. Difficulties present us with champion-refining moments. It starts with controlling the controllable.

As discussed in chapter four, in 1991 Michael Jordan, the leader and star player of the Bulls franchise, implemented a "no complaining rule." Each player was prohibited from complaining to officials, coaches, and other players. This requires control, single-mindedness, and choosing to respond instead of reacting. Reacting is negative behavior. It's an ill-advised reply to the circumstances. A response is positive. It's a well-thought-out reply to a situation.

The entire roster made great strides mentally, which impacted their physical performance. The no complaining rule created a sense of ownership, shifting the team's focus to *what they could control*, which is the exact mindset needed to build and sustain a championship culture.

Implementations of a no complaining rule in the workplace can be just as impactful. This directive removes excuses and grumbling over the uncontrollable. Doing so encourages us to concentrate solely on the things we can control and builds an uncommon level of ownership. We must starve our distractions and feed our focus, concentrating only on responsibilities, effort, and the vision. Taking pride in the things we can control allows us to create momentum when our energy is disrupted.

Some may say, "Well, expectations are different in the workplace." I disagree. In both athletics and the corporate space there is an intention to win, which requires execution. It is imperative that we cultivate an environment that is conducive for much needed growth. Having played at the college level, I understood that my coach's livelihood was dependent on our performance. At the professional level, if I had three humanly average games consecutively, I could have been replaced. As CEOs, coaches, employees, and athletes, our credibility often depends on our performance. It is imperative that we narrow our focus to what we can control to avoid wasted energy.

ACT: Circle of Success

Here's a phrase you have probably heard before: Show me your friends and I will show you your future. This has to be one of the truest things ever said. The biggest decision you will ever make is who becomes part of your circle of success. As we discussed in chapter 4, the company you keep can be the #1 asset to your success or the #1 liability. It is important to be accountable for those you allow in your space. You will become the people you spend the most time with. If they are complainers, quitters, partiers, small dreamers, subconsciously you will pick up those same habits. Your *circle of success* should be built strategically with go-getters, thrivers, and big dreamers who lead with their actions, and with like-minded influencers who will help you confront breakdowns, recognize progress, create focus, and encourage action. A circle without accountability substitutes enabling for support, and yes-men get mistaken for friends. Be sure that people in your circle of success will give you truth over harmony. As you seek growth, meet with the group or someone from the circle weekly, sharing your commitments, progress, and breakdowns.

No one is entirely self-made. Success does not come without education, equipment, or empowerment from others.

ACT: Daily Charge Up

A young soldier fights hard. A wise soldier fights smart.

Something that has served me wisely is my daily charge up. Each morning I journal, writing down how I will attack my day and rise above my former self. For younger athletes, this means focusing on your education, your Fab 5, and training. Find one area in your life that requires attention and start there. Your daily charge up can be 10-25 minutes of writing to discuss areas of your life where you want to be better.

Consistency is extremely important. You must complete this daily exercise at the beginning or at the end of your day, never in the middle of the day. Opportunities would have already been missed by that time. You want to commit to your best self *before* you begin your day to maximize each chance to be better.

Quote/Scripture – If it's not obvious, I love quotes. For me, they can serve as a boost or charge up. You are everything you read and watch. Take time daily to read a powerful quote or devotional passage or watch a video that speaks to the person you aspire to be. Find words that empower you to defeat your former self. Unpack what those words signify to you and how you will add that meaning to your life as you journal.

Commitment – Often, I take a code directly from my *CHAMPIONS' Creed*. There are sections of my creed that I can apply to anything I face in my day-to-day life. This is why it is important to know your strengths and stretches so that you can commit to who you need to be well before the moment arises when you are faced with a challenging situation. Write your commitment boldly, unapologetically, and optimistically.

Affirmation – Speak power and words of positivity in your life. Provide three words that will describe you throughout your day and that will explain what you can do to impact your results.

Opportunity – Share moments in your day that provide opportunities for growth. Maybe it's getting up earlier and being more productive. It can be how you approach extra gym time—something you know you need to do but it poses a challenge for you. Sometimes it's just two words; e.g., "Humble Yourself." Decide in advance how you will show up in those moments.

Celebration – Celebrate something you did yesterday that deserves acknowledgment (examples: completing your task list, connecting with four people). Be sure you don't skip this part of your daily charge up. It is vital to celebrate wins even if they are small. You are making strides towards your better self; celebrate your growth.

Goal – Last but certainly not least, write down one short-term and one long-term goal. This is your daily reminder of what you are working towards. Maybe it's winning your region this quarter or season, improving in three areas as a transformational leader, or growing your business by 22 clients over the next 30 days. Be specific and remember to think big. If your goals don't scare you, then you aren't thinking big enough.

The more often you do your daily charge up, you will realize the magnitude of your habits. Success begins with ownership. We must control the habits we have to achieve the results we desire.

Key Questions: Growth Mindset

Think of an area or situation in your life that requires your intentional focus right now, an area where you have fallen short and wish to close the gap. It can be personal, educational, or professional. Once you find an area of focus, answer these three questions.

1. What role did I play in this outcome?
2. What can I do to rectify this situation?
3. What can I do to prevent this from happening again?

Ownership is choosing to transform your
adversity and pain into power.

CHAMPIONS' Code: Champions avoid blame and excuses by controlling the controllable. We own our approach, our effort, our standards, our ego, the people we allow into our space, the negative behaviors we nurture, and our lack of self-honesty. We are willing to be accountable for our actions, both good and bad, in an effort to be our best. When our actions require change, we own them and make the necessary changes by asking ourselves the grand question: What can I do better to achieve the results I seek?

8
NOBILITY
THE CHAMPION'S HEART

Champions are noble in their actions and spirit. They carry themselves with great magnanimity and prestige. A noble mind is one of fine personal qualities or high moral principles and ideals. They are both formidable and true to the code of humility, dignity, and integrity. Noble minds do not seek superiority. Moral bigness is not found in anyone else's smallness; it is defined by an upright way of living. Noble is the heart of the champion.

True nobility stems from striving to rise beyond your former self, not from being superior to any other person.

Champions don't have to be business moguls, sports stars, or athletes. Sometimes you can find one in the house next door.

One summer my mother decided to move her children to the city's west side. The neighborhood was considered safer, so for the first time in my life I was allowed to stay out a little later as long as I was within earshot of my mother's voice when she called for me. I ventured out on the first day we arrived at our new home. We lived just three blocks from my new school. As I wandered nearby, I spotted a number of bikes left in front yards and knew the neighborhood must have plenty of children. I recognized immediately that things were different here. In our former neighborhood, you could never leave your bike out for any amount of time, let alone overnight, unless you just didn't want it—a lesson I had learned the hard way.

On my way back inside, I noticed our new neighbors had a basketball hoop mounted over their paved driveway. My eyes lit up. Basketball was my first love. I wondered if they would mind if I took a few shots every once in a while. I didn't want to be a pest, so I decided never to ask.

Each day I went outside and bounced my basketball on our uneven grass out back. One afternoon a man in a black pickup truck pulled into the driveway where the basketball hoop was. In the bed of the truck were wooden planks. He got out and began unloading them. He appeared to be a handy man and reminded me of Wilson W. Wilson from *Home Improvement*. I later found out his name was Ron. I watched him, and every day he would build around his home and tend to his flowers while working in and out of his shed.

I eventually realized that he and his wife were empty nesters. All of their children had gone off to college and only visited occasionally. I figured, well, that hoop isn't being used. Someone needs to use it. A few days later, I convinced my brothers of that, and we jumped on it. Before we knew it, we were drenched in sweat in an all-out pick-up game. As we were playing, that same black truck pulled into the driveway. A part of me wanted to run because I hadn't asked if we could play on our neighbor's hoop, but I realized we were caught. We lived right next door. There was no hiding from this intrusion. I stood there ashamed and ready to be corrected.

Ron pulled up and rolled down his window. He smiled and asked, "Who's winning?"

We all laughed and everyone's hands shot up.

Before parking his truck, he ended the conversation by saying, "You guys can play here any time."

That was the green light I had prayed for. I shot on that goal every day from that moment forward—often multiple times a day. I was still shooting hoops at ten, eleven, and twelve o'clock at night over the summer. I convinced myself that it wasn't too late, and I would dribble a little softer and miss less often so I didn't kick up too much ruckus. When my mother eventually called for me, I sprinted home right away.

One evening, my mother, Ron, and his wife were outside. My mother was complimenting the couple on the moonflowers they had planted in their front yard. Ron explained that their blooms opened at night. I thought that was amazing, so I checked on them nearly every evening and shared their unique blossoming process with my friends.

Days later we pulled into our driveway and discovered that Ron had planted the same flowers around the tree in our front yard. My mom couldn't believe it. I remember thinking how thoughtful that was of him. I watched Ron interact with his family and work around his house. His energy and heart were the same even when he thought no one else was looking. His generosity and magnanimous approach seemed second nature.

Because Ron allowed me to play on his basket like it was my own, I made sure all the neighborhood kids stayed off his beautiful lawn. Each year, whether spring or fall, his front and back yard looked like the botanical gardens. I was his personal security guard and was paid in jump shots.

After a Saturday full of errands, we arrived home. I helped Mom get the groceries inside, grabbed my basketball, and headed to Ron's house. As usual, I cut through our back yard. As soon as I exited the back door, I saw something that was not supposed to be in our yard. I ran into the house to get my mom and older brothers.

I screamed, "Come outside; right now! Hurry!"

They followed me to the back door. There it stood with the perfect 10-foot frame, the old school backboard with its orange square, a pure white net, and just enough cement planted to stabilize the wooden beam. I was in shock. I approached the basketball hoop and touched it as if it were a foreign object. Near tears, I looked over my shoulder. Ron and his wife stood on their back porch, smiling. They waved and went back into their house. Why would he do something so grand for a pesky kid who had been running around the neighborhood for over two years?

Ron changed my life. I don't know if he did it because he was tired of hearing my basketball bouncing late at night or if he wanted to fan my fire, but I would like to believe it was the latter. It was simply who he was, a champion, high-minded, selfless, and morally good.

My first regulation-sized hoop! I practiced on it every day. Ron built the hoop just on the other side of a power line, so I had to shoot with the perfect arc for accuracy. I eventually dribbled enough to level our back lawn, and my mother wasn't upset at all about her grass, which became nonexistent.

I credit Ron for the jump shot that made my career. But he gave me far more than a basketball hoop. Ron's selfless gesture elevated not only my game but my perspective. It taught me discipline and, more importantly, it taught me a champion's nobility. He showed me how to live my daily life with integrity even when others are not watching. He taught me to give to others, expecting absolutely nothing in return and how to stay rooted in my ideals.

The CHAMPION'S Heart

When I contemplate a champion's noble heart, I think of Evander Holyfield, a four-time heavyweight boxing champion of the world who was despised for not being an obnoxious, boisterous boxer like many of his counterparts. Even as a world champion, critics questioned his dominance because he carried himself differently. Instead of giving in to negative societal norms, he stayed rooted in the code. His mother raised him to carry himself with respect, humility, and good will. Those roots made him the only boxer to win the heavyweight championship four separate times.

Nobility also makes me think of one of my favorite childhood movies, *The Lion King*. Mufasa was my favorite character. He was the king who fought his scheming brother to maintain moral conduct on the jungle's throne. Though he and his brother had different beliefs, Mufasa still treated him with great respect. Mufasa never allowed his personal feelings or ego to get in the way of the overall vision of elevating the community he led. It was never a battle for power but a fight for what was right. His character reminds us of the type of leader we need to be even when we are in a position of power. Nobility is a way of living.

ACT: Living on Purpose, Part II

1. What are you willing to die for? This is exactly what you should be living for. Take

the time to share one issue in the world that tugs at your spirit. It may be human rights, starving children, or veteran's services. There is no cause too small if it's for the betterment of us all.

2. What can you do right now to support the cause? Financial support is only one way to move a project forward. There are many other options like advocating, volunteering your time, or using your platform to educate those within your reach.

3. ACT unapologetically while moving with purpose. This is the ultimate form of nobility. There is someone in need of your assistance and others in need of your guidance.

"Lord, let me choose the harder right instead of the easier wrong." These were the words of three-time World Champion and five-time National Champion Duke Head Coach Mike Krzyzewski as he spoke on the social injustice black and brown people in this country face daily. Coach K explained that these words were from the cadet's prayer that he recited daily when he attended West Point.

We have to choose to do what is right even when it is hard. Sadly, nobility is uncommon today—so much so that noble acts often force us to question a person's motives initially. Our responsibility as champions is to make such acts the new norm and not the exception.

To be great, you must live in a way that demands an explanation.

Key Questions: Noble Heart

1. Who are you committed to being when no one else is looking?

2. What are you willing to do for someone anonymously, not seeking acknowledgment or celebration?

3. What will you practice daily to add value to the world?

CHAMPIONS' Code: Champions live in such a way that it attracts the attention of others, forcing them to question what makes a champion so special. We carry ourselves in a way that challenges others to walk with the same prestige and honor. We avoid superiority at home and in the workplace. Instead, we seek to selflessly elevate our families, counterparts, teams, and communities.

9
SERVICE
LIVE

There is an unfortunate number of people who never get to *live* before they die. They dedicate their entire lives to money, trophies, credit, and other tangible things in an attempt to prove they existed. You will never see a U-Haul truck following a hearse. The things of this world fade away as soon as the casket is closed. Living is much more than simply being alive. It means using our passions and purpose to foster a lifestyle of success that transforms the lives of others. This requires us to think outside of our comfort zones. The greater the vision, the greater the transformation.

Throughout my life journey, I have learned that there is a special group of people that I am purposed to serve. These people connect to my experiences and my vision in a unique way. This is why the universe demands that we play big in every avenue we explore. Our influence is just as great as that of those we most admire. It is our responsibility to provide service that educates, equips, and empowers those around us. Champions live on *purpose*.

LIVE is an acronym that breaks down the significance of service: Legacy, Integrity, Value, and Efficiency.

> "The best way to find yourself is to lose yourself in the service of others." — Mahatma Gandhi

Legacy

Legacy is the blueprint that you leave behind to elevate those who come after you, the directions you hand down to teach generational wealth to your children, grandchildren, and all of your descendants. Your legacy also may be the guide you leave for your employees as they continue to build the Fortune 500 company that you founded, the standards of excellence you set within the teams you were a part of, and the people you empowered at the shelter where you volunteered. The students' lives you changed at the school where you served as an educator or the jobs you created in your community could be the lasting effects of your time in this life. Those seeds planted will be passed along to impact the lives of countless generations. What is the legacy that you are creating today?

On May 21, 2017, media trailblazer and billionaire Oprah Winfrey delivered the commencement address at Smith College. While empowering hundreds of graduates, she shared what she called the true secret to her success. Graduates, educators, relatives, and media sat at the edge of their seats awaiting this billion-dollar secret. "The power of service," she explained.

How satisfying was that for those expecting investment strategies or esoterica she had never shared on her 4,561 episodes of *The Oprah Winfrey Show*, a program anchored in the elevation of people worldwide and remaining the highest-rated television show in American history? She continued to explain that, when she decided she would only produce shows that supported her truth, she saw her greatest success. Her focus was service through passion, and, by honoring that emphasis, she became one of the wealthiest people on the planet.

Do not believe that living a life of service must be boring, unfruitful, or lacking in success. When we stand firmly in our purpose, the universe will provide the tools we need, presenting us with jewels we could not have imagined in the process.

Like yours, Oprah's journey was far from smooth. Growing up, she was a victim of sexual abuse that led to becoming pregnant at age 14. Her child passed away just two weeks after being born prematurely. Through all of this, Oprah still managed to graduate from high school with honors, earn a full scholarship to college, and eventually create her OWN network. Her network allowed her to build a platform of healing which aligned with her testimony and purpose.

She was told by her first boss that she was too emotional and not fit for television. She continued to live out her truth of service by providing resources for others. With her platform of service, Oprah made history. In 2011, she became the best-paid female in the entertainment industry and remains the richest self-made woman and only black female self-made billionaire.

As a trailblazer you must create a path never before walked. Through service, Oprah has cleared a path for millions. Use her story as fuel and directions to follow. When you lead with your why, you will find your way. Even while alive, Oprah shares a legacy of perseverance, dignity, and service.

Losses and failures do not tarnish your legacy. The treasures of growth are more often found in losing than in success. In life, working with the negatives can make for better pictures. Those obstacles are the very thing that make you great and your legacy greater. It must be *lived* daily to impact others tomorrow. It is a gift that will continue to give.

Your story will be the guide that someone else uses, not just to survive but to thrive.

Integrity

Champions have a strict ethical and moral code. Integrity is a characteristic that does not come with a specific age. It comes with a keen sense of what is right and stands firmly on this code always. It is outstanding truth, which could not have been better defined than when two global pandemics arose parallel in occurrence.

First, the worldwide pandemic of COVID-19. From January 21, 2020 to November 1, 2020, the Center of Disease Control and Prevention stated over 8.2 million cases of the coronavirus were reported worldwide. The virus spread like wildfire, killing over 220,000 people in the United States alone. The world seemed to be fragmented into opposing groups: the citizens who self-quarantined, those who doubted the severity of this pandemic, and others who questioned the validity of the powers that be.

In the midst of these unprecedented times, a woman noticed two neighborhood kids putting on a cello concert from the patio of their elderly neighbor who was self-isolating. A nine-year-old young man and his six-year-old sister arrived at their 78-year-old neighbor's house with their polished cellos in hand. The duo came neatly pressed in a suit and dress to put on an impromptu porch concert for their elderly neighbor amid the coronavirus pandemic. Their self-quarantining, classical music loving neighbor had not left her home for five days. The well-tuned two-person orchestra was caught in the act by a fellow neighbor as they played gracefully more than the required six feet away from their one-woman audience. Like flowers in May, the beautiful sound of Bach hummed through their neighborhood reminding us all that compassion is free. In unprecedented times, uprightness is magnified and even more needed.

The second pandemic is one that has plagued our world's history for hundreds of years. Racism has been more than just a blemish in US history. The social injustices that minorities face regularly taint the history of this country and continue to plague our society. An injustice to one is an injustice to all.

On August 26, 2016, in an effort to change our entire world for the better, San Francisco Quarterback Colin Kaepernick knelt during the National Anthem of a televised NFL game to bring awareness to social injustice: the oppression of people of color and police brutality. He used his voice to share a message of equality. This caused an uproar as many mistook his peaceful protest as disrespect to the flag and the great people who have served as soldiers for our nation. He was crucified on social media and eventually exiled from the NFL. Despite the backlash, Kaepernick continued to display integrity by using his platform and his voice to fight for the voiceless. He stood and even knelt for what is right and not what was easy. While ranked as one of the best quarterbacks in the NFL, he did this at the expense of his career. There is no greater service than to sacrifice of yourself for the elevation of someone else.

> "I know of no great man except those who have rendered great services to the human race."
> Voltaire

It takes true integrity to sit for civil rights as Rosa Parks did, to walk for freedom like Dr. Martin Luther King, to fight for equality like Bruce Lee, or to kneel against racial injustice like Colin Kaepernick. It requires greatness to challenge the status quo as Steve Kerr has done and as did his father Malcom Kerr, who died for it. There is nothing more heroic than fighting for what is right and standing for those oppressed. In fact, this is heroism defined.

Justice and poverty will not be changed until those unaffected or in positions of power are as outraged as those affected. Like Batman, Storm, and Black Panther, it requires clarity of vision, courage, and integrity to advocate for those oppressed. This is a service that each of us can provide.

> "I prefer to be true to myself, even at the hazard
> of incurring the ridicule of others, rather than
> to be false, and to incur my own abhorrence."
> Frederick Douglass

Value

In 2013 I founded the Max-OUT Foundation. Our mission at Max-OUT is to *"Maximize Opportunity, Unity, and Training"* in our communities. We meet weekly keeping this mission at the forefront while creating new ways to provide invaluable services for others. In one of our Max-OUT Foundation staff reads, *The Go-Giver*, Bob Burg and John David Mann break down *The Five Laws of Stratospheric Success*. The #1 law is the "Law of Value." Your true worth is determined by how much more you give in value than you receive in payment. People with an average mindset would not understand this business model. Unfortunately, most businesses have a goal to give the least in value for the most in return.

Here is a short excerpt from *The Go-Giver*:

> *All great fortunes in the world have been created by men or women who had a greater passion for what they were giving—their product, service or idea—than for what they were getting. And many of those great fortunes have been squandered by others who had a greater passion for what they were getting than what there were giving. The majority of people operate with a mindset that says to the fireplace, 'First give me some heat, then I'll throw on some logs.' Or that says to the bank, 'Give me interest on my money, then I'll make a deposit.' And of course, it just doesn't work that way. You give, give, give. Why? Because you love to. It's not strategy, it's a way of life.*

The journey to becoming a champion is about refining, and the list of names who have reached that status is short. To be among the champions in your respected industry, your intention must be first to provide invaluable value as leaders, associates, players, and coaches. So often we seek the promotion for tenure and not significance. Do more than what is expected.

As a player or associate, to add value, we must star in our role. Know the value of your role and strive to exceed expectations with your daily effort and energy. An example would be supporting others on your team genuinely, not only because it serves but because it's who you are. Make it clear why you are on that team or in that organization. As an influencer, live in a way that positively impacts the direction of the team or organization. Serve unselfishly and beyond your job description. Develop the habit of setting standards that others will be measured by. Finally, give unselfishly. Selfless acts are forms of service. Be willing to let go of self to assure the success of those around you. In return, everyone wins.

The greatest thing you can do today is
anything you do for someone else.

Efficiency

Life is like a spades game. Spades is a card game I played as a child. There are many variations, but I grew up playing one in which aces were the highest cards, face cards were the second highest, and spades were the strongest suit. After you are dealt your hand, it is up to you to make that hand as efficient and effective as possible. There are two types of spades' players when it comes to being dealt a hand that challenges you to play with more thought, strategy, and efficiency. You have the person who loses before the first card is played. They don't like the cards they receive, so they give up. This kind of person sees the frustration that comes with challenge and allows annoyance to win. He or she views competition as a hinderance and folds. The second kind of player is rare. They can do more with less and play with the same level of commitment no matter the hand they are dealt.

The same is true in business and on a sports team. When the odds are low, the second kind of person puts on his or her hard hat and attempts to dig for more. These people see challenge as an opportunity to show off their greatness and their ability to thrive at a rare level in less than ideal circumstances. They choose to succeed, not just to survive. This makes them highly sought out by businesses and teams because this energy is contagious. It serves in a way that elevates the entire group much like the drive exhibited by the greats that have been featured in this book.

The best spades' player I ever knew was my great grandmother, whom I called GG. She and I never played cards together, but she could make a dollar out of two cents and was a master of efficiency. She made a living in industrial laundry and as a housekeeper. She would put the finest hotels to shame with her wrinkleless bed sheets and dustless home décor. She was born and raised in the backwoods and on the dirt roads of Ferriday, Louisiana. Having no more than an eighth-grade education before entering the workforce, she spent a lot of her life making minimum wage or less. In the 1950s she moved to Chicago to complete her general education development and became a certified seamstress for a world-renowned suit company—all while taking care of her family as a widow. After her passing, she left my family with a legacy of determination and efficiency. These same principles were passed along to me.

Her legacy instilled in me an approach to give nothing less than my best. A desire to do more and be more despite the cards we are dealt is a great service to our families, teams, and humanity.

ACT: Servanthood

Servants find opportunities to maximize their service. To grow in our service as leaders, we must do three things extremely well:

1. Zoom out - Champions think, move, and live beyond themselves.
2. Anticipate opportunity – Eagerly seek opportunities to support others using the resources you have.
3. ACT with genuine compassion – Action creates transformation.

As you navigate life as an athlete or a professional, what will you make out of the cards you are dealt? How will this efficiently serve others? We were placed on the Earth to do so much more than win and die.

A popular hymn GG often sang was "This Little Light of Mine." The lyrics go, "I'm going to let it shine, let it shine, let it shine." When GG sang that tune, she was reminding herself to let her God-given light shine brightly everywhere she went and regardless of the circumstances.

Like a candle that lights another candle, champions use their flame to spark the wick of others. Your light will shine more luminously when you serve others. That is what it means to LIVE, working every day to leave an eternal legacy, acting with the integrity of world greats, seeking to add value in a way that is invaluable, and living efficiently to maximize your greatest potential. True champions *live on purpose.*

Key Questions: The Circle of Life

1. Reflect on your obituary exercise from chapter 6. On the day that you expire, what will have been your most rewarding accomplishment?

2. How will this achievement impact those around you?

3. What are you doing now to educate, equip, and empower those you influence to live out your legacy today?

CHAMPIONS' Code: A champion's success is not determined by where that person is now. It's defined by how far someone has come and those who were helped along the way. Our duty as champions is to use our experiences to provide guidance for those we are fortunate to serve now and leave clear directions for those who come after us. We do this by choosing what is right over what is comfortable to maximize our uncommon abilities. Champions LIVE.

10
CHAMPIONS' CREED

Your greatness has been activated! We have unpacked the nine essential qualities that define world-class champions, breaking down what each letter represents: Character, Honor, Adversity, Mindset, Preparation, Influence, Ownership, Nobility and Service. You have now discovered what it takes and who you need to be in order to reach uncommon results. The MAP (Mindset, Approach, and Performance) you created by reading and actively completing the first nine chapters of this book will jump start your personal life, your team, and your career and will elevate your success.

You may be asking, "But, Marke, where do I go from here?" You can have all the correct ingredients for your favorite meal, but, if you don't apply each properly, you will be disappointed when it is time to sit down and indulge. From this moment it is important to move with great intention and accountability.

Start now! As we have discussed multiple times in this book, you do not have to be perfect, but you must be consistent. *LIVE* out each word of your *CHAMPIONS' Creed.* Stay true to each promise in the code and relentlessly pursue excellence. Your results will follow your efforts.

Are you ready to vow to yourself that you will honor the champions' creed? If you are willing, then read and sign the creed below and do your best to abide by these truths each day.

CHAMPIONS' Creed

Champion status is not achieved in the moment, but long before, when I decide to do what is necessary to become great. I make this decision daily in each moment to continue to practice greatness and to choose to be the best version of myself. The development of my character is where my success lies. The rewards, promotion, profit, and trophies I may receive are not the attainment of the champion I am but simply confirmation of it.

I take pride in succeeding, not winning. I lose and win with great honor and integrity. This allows me to succeed even when the results are not in my favor. I approach each task with a magnanimous heart, a grateful spirit, and the strength to overcome. It is not a prize that is most valuable. What is most important is who I become and those I assist along the way.

My past does not define me. It refines me. My pain has been transformed into fuel. I know that I cannot be who I aspire to be without those transformational moments. As a champion, I make the conscious effort to thrive when adversity is presented, allowing each moment to grow me mentally and prepare me for my greater good. I will step back, step up, and step forward, for my purpose is much bigger than my pain.

I control my thoughts which dictate my actions and directly impact my results. I am confident because I have earned the right to live the role of a champion through meticulous preparation and optimistic visualization. I am my greatest competition; I challenge myself to be better. I am also my #1 fan, undoubtedly believing in my abilities and my destiny. My mindset is my greatest asset.

My effort is never in question. I show I care by how I prepare — with a student's approach and a surgeon's precision, not mistaking activity for productivity. I am deliberate with each action because of my commitment to my better self. I respect the process, understanding that the dream is free, but the hustle is sold separately. My pursuit of excellence is incomparable and undeniable.

My influence is invaluable. I lead, not for selfish gain but for the growth and success of my team, understanding that the best way to lead is by example. I leave each person I come in contact with better than they were before I met them. Though a leader, I am an outstanding follower. I do not allow my ego to get in the way of the vision.

I avoid blame and excuses by controlling what I can. I own my approach, my effort, my standards, my ego, the people I allow in my space, the behaviors I nurture, and my narrative. I am willing to be accountable for my actions, both good and bad, in an effort to be my best. When my actions require change, I self-reflect and correct.

I live in such a way that I set the standards that others will be measured by. I carry myself in a way

*that challenges others to walk with the same prestige
and nobility. I avoid superiority, not mistaking it for
leadership. Instead, I seek to selflessly elevate my family,
counterparts, and community.*

*My success as a champion is not dictated by where I am
now. It's determined by how far I have come and by those
I served along the way. My duty is to use my experiences
to provide guidance for those I am fortunate to lead now
and leave clear directions for those who come after me.
I do this by choosing what is right over what is easy to
maximize my unique abilities.*

Champion's Signature _____

Date: _____

By signing your champion's creed, you have committed to the person you aspire to be. Place these principles where you can revisit them regularly for accountability, and vow to apply these powerful strategies to your daily life.

As we discussed in the introduction of this book, champions are acknowledged for their accomplishments but defined by their daily habits. Your mission starts with your commitment—a conscious decision to be your very best to achieve your very best.

Thank you for taking this journey with me. It is our first but surely will not be our last.

I would love to hear how you continue to apply the concepts that have been introduced in the *CHAMPIONS' Creed* to champion your life. I invite you to share your success stories with others at www.MarkeFreemanMedia.com/ChampionsCreed.

Remember, success is not defined by where you are now. It is determined by who you choose to be, how far you have come, and those you help along the way.

Your fellow champion,

Marke Z. Freeman

ACKNOWLEDGMENTS

It truly takes a village. *CHAMPIONS' Creed* would not have even been an idea if it weren't for the love and support of my tribe.

I want to thank my grandparents whom I was ever so blessed to have in my life from my earliest memories well into adulthood. My great grandmother Annie "GG" Willingham exemplified strength and perseverance. My grandmother Charlene Anderson taught me that beauty transcends from within. My Grandmother Edna Freeman embodied boldness and strong-mindedness. And my Grandfather Alfonso Young never missed a game due to rain, sleet, or snow and always told me how special I was. They were my championship team. Though they have since transitioned, they still LIVE in me, and the wisdom they shared played a major role in the writing of *CHAMPIONS' Creed*. I am forever grateful for the immeasurable love and irreplaceable memories.

Marke Z. Freeman

I offer profound gratitude to Ma, my favorite coach, the most resilient and selfless being I know, my mother Racine Freeman. The older I get, the better I understand the sacrifices you made for each of your children as a single mother. Without your steady hand and unconditional love, I would not be who I am today. You are my shero. Thank you for allowing me the freedom to be who I am and never limiting who I can become.

To my siblings, Jesse, Jamie, Rhavan, Tosha, Jahmal, Darius, James, and Lisa, where do I begin? You are my first friends, my protectors, and my examples. Thank you for your guidance, unbelievable memories, and unquestioned love and support.

Dubby, you have been the answer to so many of my questions, the shoulder for many of my tears, and the inspiration behind much of my recent success. Thank you for keeping me grounded yet lifted.

A special thank you goes to LaChina Robinson. As my mentor, you have taught me what it means to reach back and pull up. Thank you for helping me grow as a woman, and thank you for being my sounding board and my truth when needed.

I also want to thank the army of women I was blessed with the discernment to choose. Each of you knows who you are and how much you mean to me. My sisters and my riders. God gave me a bunch of brothers because he knew we would find each other. Thank you for being my voices of reason and my good times.

I have to thank every coach I have had from my earliest years to my professional career. Your role was not restricted to the sideline. You have served as mentors, parental figures, confidants, and so much more. Thank you for not giving up on me when I probably made it easy to. Thank you for celebrating me and challenging me to be my best in all areas of my life.

Then there are my teammates. I laugh or cry nearly every time I reminisce about our time together. As much as I appreciate the big wins, those games will never replace our sisterhood. Thank you for having my back, front, and sides.

To my Springfield community, Cox Park, and the east side that raised me, I acknowledge that it takes a village. Ubuntu, a term used in South Africa, means I am what I am because of who we all are. Thank you.

A heartfelt thank you to my support team of endorsers. You all have played a special role at pivotal points in my life. Thank you for educating, equipping, and empowering me to fulfill my life's purpose.

Thank you to my board of editors, who helped me bring this book to life: Mrs. Seifert, Jayson, Cheetara, and Kenneth. Thank you for your time, energy, and insights shared.

In addition, I want to thank my Book Coach Cathy Fyock for your resourcefulness and commitment to making the world a better place one word at a time.

To my editor, fellow basketball fanatic, Diana Henderson, for your prowess, patience, and handling of my vision with a champion's care, thank you.

My appreciation goes to my cover designer, Michael Scott, for his ridiculously amazing attention to detail, bringing the face of my project to life.

I thank my formatter, Drew Becker, for his outstanding knowledge and for assisting me through the final steps in the completion of CHAMPIONS' Creed.

To my publishing company Lighthouse Press, thank you for helping me give birth to my first child. I can now say that I am very proud mother.

And, finally, I want to thank the rest of my amazing family, friends, and fans that I have encountered on my life journey, those who helped me grow, those who remained open to the knowledge I had to share, and those who pushed me through. Thank you for your continued love and support. I am eternally gratefully to all who have helped me discover my inner *champion*.

ABOUT THE AUTHOR

Marke Freeman is a former professional basketball player and a world-renowned speaker. She reaches thousands through corporate performance coaching and transformational keynote presentations that provide execution strategies by educating, equipping, and empowering individuals and organizations worldwide. Marke serves business entities, leaders, students, and athletes globally, instilling mental foundations for success and motivation to achieve high-level results and, more importantly, providing the actionable methods that will enable others to grow and thrive through leadership, mindset, habits, personal success, and culture transformation. Marke introduces undeniable strategies that world-class athletes use to perform at a championship level, which can be utilized in business to build and sustain a winning culture and in life to discover your inner CHAMPION.

Born September 20, 1988, Marke was raised in a single parent home on the east side of Springfield, Illinois. She has faced many forms of adversity making them the acme of her testimony. Her story is one of Commitment, Accountability, Perseverance, and Evolution, which she refers to as CAPE because this approach saved her life.

With her audiences, Marke shares her message of trials, tribulations, and triumph. Her story is proof that success is about combating victimization and seeking ownership—committing to the process and not just seeking results. It's about starving one's distractions and feeding one's focus to ensure growth while performing at your highest level despite challenging circumstances.

This stalwart attitude served Marke well throughout her career. She graduated high school with honors, receiving a full academic/athletic scholarship to attend and play basketball in college. She had an exceptional career at Northern Illinois University, earning her an opportunity to travel the world to play professional basketball. Her academic, athletic, and professional accomplishments did not come without challenges, failures, setbacks, and comebacks. She cherishes each experience because this was the formula needed to discover her inner CHAMPION.

Marke has served as a women's basketball college coach, helping lead programs to the NCAA tournament on multiple occasions, even making it to the Elite Eight in the national tournament. She also serves as a sports analyst, interviewing and studying the greatest sports' minds in the world. She ties her passion for sports, impact, and leadership into her mission to build champions on and off the court.

Aside from her athletic success, Marke always believed in championing life beyond basketball, and her most fulfilling accomplishment is founding the Max-OUT Foundation. Max-OUT is a nonprofit organization with a mission to "**Max**imize **O**pportunity, **U**nity and **T**raining" in communities by influencing positive life choices. This results in reduced truancy and increases the retention rate by teaching purpose, leadership development, and mindset needed to achieve greatness. Max-OUT has impacted the lives of thousands throughout the United States and abroad.

Marke has led various conferences, written a book, and has had countless speaking engagements. She has equipped and educated thousands through her dynamic and thought-provoking teaching and empowerment of corporate professionals, teams, our youth of today and leaders of tomorrow. Truly living through her world, Marke is a leader, CEO, founder, author, motivational speaker, sports analyst, athlete, skill development coach, and humanitarian. Ms. Freeman is not done yet. She continues to innovate ways to enhance the lives of others and lead them in a clearer direction, instilling value and passion in each person. She is uncommon. But once you get to know her, you will learn she is an ordinary woman with an extraordinary message that has shifted the trajectory of many lives.

Marke Z. Freeman

For more on Marke visit her website:
www.MarkeFreemanMedia.com.

To contact her directly, email her at:
Marke@MarkeFreemanMedia.com.

Stay Connected:

LinkedIn: Marke Freeman

Facebook: https://www.facebook.com/MarkeFree

Instagram: instagram.com/markefree

Twitter: twitter.com/markefree